THE GUIDE OF ALL GUIDES

ANGELIQUE FAWNS

Copyright © 2021 by angelique fawns

All rights reserved.

No part of this book may be reproduced in any form or by any electronic or mechanical means, including information storage and retrieval systems, without written permission from the author, except for the use of brief quotations in a book review.

This guide is intended to help writers, but does not guarantee complete accuracy after the date of publication as writing markets are fluid. The order of markets presented in this guide is in no way a reflection or comment on their value or importance.

The opinions expressed in this publication are those of the authors. They do not purport to reflect the opinions or views of any market within it.

Cover design based on original artwork by Rong Hu

❀ Created with Vellum

This book is dedicated to all the wonderful magazine, podcast, and ezine publishers providing opportunities for writers worldwide.

CONTENTS

Preface ix

PART I
MAGAZINES
1. The Magazine of Fantasy & Science Fiction 3
2. Clarkesworld 7
3. Uncanny 11
4. Asimov's Science Fiction 13
5. Unreal/Unfit Magazines 17
6. Diabolical Plots 21
7. On Spec 25
8. Strange Horizons 29
9. Analog Science Fiction and Fact 33
10. Amazing Stories 37
11. Apex Magazine 41
12. Beneath Ceaseless Skies 43
13. Mysterion 47
14. Fantasy Magazine 51
15. Nightmare Magazine 53
16. Lightspeed Magazine 57
17. Deep Magic 59
18. Ellery Queen Mystery Magazine 63
19. Alfred Hitchcock Mystery Magazine 67
20. The Reckoning 71
21. Cossmass Infinities 75
22. DreamForge Anvil 79
23. Cosmic Roots & Eldritch Shores 83
24. The Dark Magazine 89
25. Abyss & Apex Magazine 91
26. Zooscape 95
27. Visions 99
28. 34 Orchard 103
29. Vasterien 107
30. Apparition Lit 111

31. Translunar Travellers Lounge	113
32. Three-Lobed Burning Eye	117
33. Lamplight	121
34. Neo-opsis Science Fiction Magazine	123
35. Interzone	125
36. Sexy Fantastic Magazine	127
37. ParABnormal	131
38. Pulp Modern	135
39. Econoclash Review	139
40. Electric Spec	143
41. Allegory	147
42. Switchblade	151
43. Novel Noctule	155
44. The House of Zolo Journal of Speculative Literature	159
45. Dark Matter Magazine	161
46. Bone Yard Soup Magazine	163
47. The Curiouser	167
48. The Common Tongue	169
49. Planet Scumm	173
50. The Weird and Whatnot	175
51. Frost Zone Zine	177
52. New Myths	179

PART II
FLASH FICTION MARKETS

53. Daily Science Fiction	183
54. Arsenika	185
55. The Arcanist	187
56. Dream of Shadows	191
57. SciPhi Journal	195
58. Flash Point Science Fiction	199

PART III
PODCASTS

59. Cast of Wonders	205
60. Podcastle	209
61. Psuedopod	211
62. Escape Pod	215
63. The Other Stories	217
64. The Overcast	221

65. NoSleep 225
66. Gallery of Curiosities 227

Acknowledgments 229
About the Author 231
Also by Angelique Fawns 233

PREFACE

"A short story is a different thing altogether – a short story is like a quick kiss in the dark from a stranger."

— STEPHEN KING

You've written your short story. Now where do you send it? This guide contains the very best markets in the speculative fiction realm. None of them charge reading fees. All of them pay their writers.

There are so many potential homes, the choices are staggering. *The Guide of all Guides* lists the TOP paying markets for speculative fiction, basically ordered with the highest-paying, most established magazines first.

Some markets pay a generous amount for the first 1,000 words then cap the total spent. Others might pay lucratively, but are so recently founded, they lack a track record or recognizable name for your credit list. Those are listed further into the book.

- How quickly do you want to hear back about your story?
- Would you like helpful hints from the editor?
- Which venue is the right place for your work?

Preface

The Guide of all Guides can help you figure out where to send that quirky tale about a vampire, your dystopian science fiction saga, or your slipstream comedy. Some places go through their slush pile in record time and send back a "yay" or "nay" almost immediately. Others can hold stories for up to a year. My favorite editors sometimes send helpful hints along with their rejections.

I've been penning my own tales since May, 2018 and over 30 of them found homes with magazines, podcasts or anthologies.

It was not an easy journey.

I collected more than 500 rejections while submitting to over 100 markets. Some took my submission, charged me to read it, and then sent me a form rejection. Others held my work for more than two years and I still haven't heard anything. I have not included markets that make you "pay to play" or suck your story into the slush pile abyss for eternity.

This guide is what I needed when I began. It will give you:

- **all the basics you need to submit**
- **introduce the market with a bit of history**
- **tell you what the editors are looking for**
- **show you the typical rejection letter**

I'm not positioning myself as an expert or guru here, preaching to new writers, and holding my accomplishments up to be admired. Rather, we are in this together, exploring the fun and frustrating world of short story publishing. I'll be frank and honest. I made $500 US in 2019 from my short stories. In 2020, I made double that.

The publishing world is a fluid one, especially for the short story market. Old established markets close their doors, like Orson Scott Card's *Intergalactic Medicine Show* in June, 2019; and new ezines and podcasts launch all the time.

This guide is not meant to showcase them ALL. (That would be impossible) But it does give a good comprehensive list of markets actively and honestly soliciting stories.

Preface

Note: the ordering in this book is in no way meant to reflect on the importance or value of each publisher.

If you find out something in this guide has changed, please drop me a line at:

- @angeliquefawns on Twitter,
- https://www.facebook.com/amfawns

Hopefully my journey can help yours.

PART I
MAGAZINES

1

THE MAGAZINE OF FANTASY & SCIENCE FICTION

Past Editor: C.C. Finlay
   Current Editor: Sheree Renee Thomas
   Pay: 8-12 cents per word
   Word range: flash to 25,000
   Simultaneous submissions? No
   Reprints? No

When it comes to helpful rejection letters, fast turnaround times, and a high-quality product, this is my favorite place to submit stories. *The Magazine of Fantasy & Science Fiction* is a Science Fiction & Fantasy Writers of America (SFWA) qualifying market based out of the United States. Founded in 1949, they produce six print issues a year.

They are the original publishers of science fiction classics

> like Stephen King's "Dark Tower" and Daniel Keyes's
> "Flowers for Algernon".

I've sent them 14 stories and received a rejection for all of them. However, five of the rejection letters included detailed reasons why C.C. Finlay did not accept them. "The Last Ride," "Camp Napanoo," "The Versa Vice," "The Writing Retreat," and "The Patron Saint of Livestock," all came back with thoughtful notes that helped me rewrite each tale and sell them to other markets.

The new (and 10th) editor for 2021, Sheree Renee Thomas, is an award-winning Pushcart-nominated author. Her work is inspired by myth, folklore, and natural science. I look forward to reading her rejections and cross my fingers there may be an acceptance eventually.

The Magazine of Fantasy & Science Fiction is frequently open to submissions and only close when they need to get on top of their slush pile.

According to the writer's guidelines:

> "Submissions have increased more than 10% this year, compared to last, and you aren't just sending us more stories, you're sending us more really excellent stories. That is one of the few good things we'll say about 2020. Give us this chance to go through them."

Another plus to this market is the rapid turnaround. I never had to wait more than two weeks to get my "nay." However, the guidelines do ask for writers to allow eight weeks for a response. Fun fact: C.C. Finlay is active on twitter and posts cool pictures of his cat. @ccfinlay

One of his (many) rejections:

> "Thank you for giving me a chance to read "The Museum of the Lost People."

> This always feels like it's on the edge of turning into a hot urban fantasy romance to me...

which is great, and I think this shows a lot of natural talent in that direction, which I mention only because I have several friends who do pretty well writing (sometimes traditional publishing, sometimes self-publishing) urban fantasy, if that's not something you're already doing. Even though I liked the ending,

> I kept wanting the narrator to take more initiative earlier in the story

I understand that holding is part of what creates the tension and drives the story, but it didn't work as well for me as I thought it needed to. In the end, this story didn't quite win me over for Fantasy & Science Fiction and I'm going to have to pass. But I thought the writing was good -- I wish you best of luck finding the right market for it and hope that you'll keep us in mind again in the future."

"The Museum of the Lost People" is still looking for a home, but I gave it a rewrite giving the protagonist more initiative and adding more of a romantic angle.

If you want to learn more about this market, Gordon Van Gelder, Publisher of *The Magazine of Fantasy & Science Fiction* gave a lecture at *Odyssey's 2014 Writing Workshop*. I've listened to it three times. It is chock full of timeless good advice.

Gordon Van Gelder Workshop

~

Submit here:
https://www.sfsite.com/fsf/glines.htm

2

CLARKESWORLD

antasy & Science Fiction

Publisher/Editor: Neil Clarke
   Pay: 10 cents per word
   Word range: 1,000 - 22,000
   Simultaneous submissions? No
   Reprints? No
   Ezine, Print & Podcast- Based out of US

Clarkesworld is an award-winning science fiction and fantasy magazine. A SFWA-qualifying market, it was first published in 2006 and is one of the top places speculative fiction writers want to see their work. It comes out monthly, and contains interviews, stories, and articles. They accept stories from all over the world and say translations are welcome. They also have a podcast which features a story from the current issue.

The submission guidelines state:

"Science fiction need not be "hard" SF, but rigor is appreciated. Fantasy can be folkloric, contemporary, surreal, etc. That said, there are some things that we've grown tired of and can be difficult or impossible to sell to us: (this is not a challenge)

- stories that include zombies or zombie-wannabes
- stories about sexy vampires, wanton werewolves, wicked witches, or demonic children
- stories about rapists, murderers, child abusers, or cannibals
- stories where the climax is dependent on the spilling of intestines
- stories in which a milquetoast civilian government is depicted as the sole obstacle to either catching some depraved criminal or to an uncomplicated military victory
- stories where the Republicans, or Democrats, or Libertarians, or ... (insert any established political party or religion here) take over the world and either save or ruin it
- stories in which the words "thou" or "thine" appear
- stories with talking cats or swords
- stories where FTL travel or time travel is as easy as is it on television shows or movies
- stories about young kids playing in some field and discovering ANYTHING. (a body, an alien craft, Excalibur, ANYTHING).
- stories about the stuff you just read in Scientific American or saw on the news
- stories about your RPG character's adventures
- "funny" stories that depend on, or even include, puns
- stories where the protagonist is either widely despised or

- widely admired simply because he or she is just so smart and/or strange
- stories originally intended for someone's upcoming theme anthology or issue (everyone is sending those out, wait a while)
- your trunk stories
- stories that try to include all of the above"

The submission window is normally open and I've found they have fast turnaround, usually within a week or so. I've had nine rejections from this market.

They give a standard letter:

"Thank you for the opportunity to read "The Metamorphosis." Unfortunately, your story isn't quite what we're looking for right now. In the past, we've provided detailed feedback on our rejections, but I'm afraid that due to time considerations, we're no longer able to offer that service. I appreciate your interest in Clarkesworld Magazine and hope that you'll keep us in mind in the future."

"The Metamorphosis" was purchased by *Scare Street* after being rejected 3 times by other markets. The editor asked for a series of edits before buying it. You can find this story about the genesis of a leech man in an upcoming anthology here:
https://scarestreet.com

Submit here:
http://clarkesworldmagazine.com/submissions/

3

UNCANNY

cience Fiction & Fantasy

Submissions Editor: Brahidaliz Martinez
  Pay: 10 cents per word
  Word range: 750-6,000
  Simultaneous submissions? Yes
  Reprints? No
  Ezine - Based out of US

Uncanny magazine specializes in stories that make you *feel*. Classifying itself as an on-line/eBook/podcast SF/F magazine, their cover art is breathtaking. It has won multiple Hugo Awards, a Parsec Award, and a British Fantasy Award. The two Editors-in-Chief; Lynne M. Thomas, and Michael Damian Thomas, have also won several Hugo Awards. It is a SFWA-qualified market.

From the website:

"Uncanny Magazine is an online Science Fiction and Fantasy magazine featuring passionate SF/F fiction and poetry, gorgeous prose, provocative nonfiction, and a deep investment in the diverse SF/F culture. Each issue contains intricate, experimental stories and poems with verve and imagination that elicit strong emotions and challenge beliefs, from writers of every conceivable background. Uncanny believes there's still plenty of room in the genre for tales that make you feel."

Lynne M. Thomas said in a reddit interview:

"For me it's not necessarily about a kind of story, it's about how the kind of story is executed.

I'm interested in stories that are inclusive of the gamut of the human experience, and I want to see a bit more whimsy."

I've submitted two stories to *Uncanny* and both times they have gotten back to me quickly with a standard rejection letter:

"Thank you for submitting "The Patron Saint of Livestock" to Uncanny Magazine for consideration. Unfortunately, we're going to pass on this one. It just didn't work for us. We look forward to reading further submissions from you."

"The Patron Saint of Livestock", a story about a dark magical chicken, has been picked up by *Cosmic Roots & Eldritch Shores*.

Submit here:
https://uncannymagazine.com/submissions/

4
ASIMOV'S SCIENCE FICTION

cience Fiction

Editor: Sheila Williams
    Pay: 8-10 cents per word
    Word range: 1,000-20,000
    Simultaneous submissions? No
    Reprints? No
    Print - Based out of US

Asimov's Science Fiction Magazine is a powerhouse in the science fiction world and was founded in 1977 by Joel Davis and Isaac Asimov. This publication is part of the Dell Magazine family and SFWA-qualified. Personally, I adore Isaac Asimov's anthologies of short stories, especially his "Robot" series.

    Their website asks:

Have you ever wondered where George R. R. Martin's Daenerys Targaryen first appeared on the printed page?

Where Kim Stanly Robinson first staked his claim on "Green Mars"? Who first published Octavia E. Butler's Hugo and Nebula Award winning short fiction? What magazine was home to the first professional fiction publications of Jonathan Lethem, Kelly Link, and Allen M. Steele? Asimov's Science Fiction Magazine, of course!"

They have a very specific request for content:

"In general, we're looking for "character oriented" stories, those in which the characters, rather than the science, provide the main focus for the reader's interest.

 Serious, thoughtful, yet accessible fiction will constitute the majority of our purchases, but there's always room for the humorous as well.

SF dominates the fiction published in the magazine, but we also publish borderline fantasy, slipstream, and surreal fiction. No sword & Sorcery, please. Neither are we interested in explicit sex or violence. A good overview would be to consider that all fiction is written to examine or illuminate some aspect of human existence, but that in science fiction the backdrop you work against is the size of the Universe."

Asimov's has a form letter they send out for rejections, and I've gotten six of them. I once got a tiny note from Sheila Williams herself at the end of one. I heard her give a lecture on the *Odyssey Writing Workshop Podcast*, and loved it, so I put a comment referencing how much I enjoyed it in one of my submissions.

"Thank you very much for letting us see "Shafted." We appreciate your taking the time to send it in for our consideration. Although it does not suit the needs of the magazine at this time, we wish you luck with placing it elsewhere. Thanks for your kind comments about my podcast. Good to know that someone found it."

"Shafted" is being turned into a paranormal romance novel.

Sheila William's Odyssey lecture

Submit here:
http://asimovs.magazinesubmissions.com

5
UNREAL/UNFIT MAGAZINES

Fantasy & Science Fiction

Editor: Daniel White Scott
  Pay: 25 cents per word for the first 1,000
  1 cent per afterwards
  Word range: under 10,000
  Simultaneous submissions? Yes
  Print & Ezine -Based out of US & Taiwan

These two magazines are imprints owned by Longshot Press and some of the highest paying in genre fiction. They are proudly not a part of the Science Fiction & Fantasy Writers of America (SFWA) organization.

Unfit Magazine is a pulp fiction style science fiction magazine with the tag line:

> "Fiction that isn't fit for 'them'! Toxic content. (Keep it secret!) We run with scissors. Banned by your Mother."

Unreal Magazine is also a pulp fiction style magazine focusing on fantasy. The tag line is:

> Let the magic take you away! Fiction that isn't made for this world. So, let go. Get unreal for a moment."

The submission pages suggest:

"We want stories that are well written, intelligent, and enjoyable to read. We are looking for stories with metaphors and emotional ambiance and imaginative descriptive writing. Most importantly, we want original ideas."

Longshot Press also has two more imprints. *Longshot Island* which focuses on psychological short stories; and *Mythaxis Review*, a platform dedicated to art and technology. This on-line magazine features articles, interviews, essays, and workshops.

The art for these magazines is absolutely gorgeous. You can connect and comment on any of these imprints at *thinkerbeat.com* and create your own page for promoting your personal writing, website and blog.

Daniel White Scott runs Longshot Press and has been a valuable contact for me in my writing journey. We started corresponding in March 2020 when I asked if I could interview him for *horrortree.com*. I am hoping to have one of my stories picked up by *Unreal* or *Unfit* but so far, I've received 13 rejections.

Scott responded:

> Thanks for the offer to do an interview. Maybe later, but I'm not interested at this time. If you would like, I have two horror publishers I would like interviewed."

Since then, I have written several interviews and articles for *Mythaxis.com*. I've repurposed some of these interviews for in-depth dives featuring publishers in *The Story Behind The Stories*, and *The Publishers Behind The Pages*. (Both of these books are a part of this series.)

Scott is actively looking for more writers who can interview and write essays featuring musicians and the music world.

～

Submit here:
    https://unrealmag.com/submit/
    https://unfitmag.com/submit/

6
DIABOLICAL PLOTS

Science Fiction, Fantasy & Horror

Editor: David Steffen
  Pay: 10 cents per word
  Word range: max 3,500
  Simultaneous submissions? No
  Reprints? No
  Ezine and Print – Based out of US

Diabolical Plots is a SWFA-qualifying market that buys speculative fiction that leans towards startling, odd, and interesting. If you have a character-driven story with a strong inner and outer arc, this maybe a good place to submit.

The editor, David Steffen, advises writers to be wary of being wordy.

"Tight concise prose that gives you everything you need to understand the story without overstaying its welcome, relatable characters, cool speculative ideas, all written very tightly. You don't have many words, there is no space to waste."

Fun fact: David Steffen is the co-founder and administrator of The Submission Grinder, a web-tool used by writers to find and log their submissions.

The website says they are looking for:

"Speculative fiction–science fiction, fantasy, and horror. Everything should have a speculative element–that includes horror. Feel free to mix in other genres at will–a fantasy mystery or a science fiction romance.
And yes, we really mean it has to have a speculative element. If you submit a serial killer story with only mundane elements, even though that could be a horror story it's not a speculative horror story and it will be rejected regardless of quality.

- Things that we tend to really like:
- Weird fiction
- Sense of wonder
- Strong character and plot arcs
- Strong world-building, hinting at more to see around the edges of the story
- Philosophical food-for-thought
- Straightforward, easily readable style
- Religion, where the story does not try to convert the reader, nor does the story demonize religion
- Platonic friendship between men and women"

The Guide of All Guides

I submitted one story to *Diabolical Plots* and this was my rejection letter,

"Thank you for allowing us to read your story, "The Patron Saint of Livestock".
Unfortunately, we are not accepting your story. Please excuse this form letter. It is not a reflection on your submission--we would love to give personal responses to every submission, but can only afford to do so for a small subset to keep response times down. (Reading on mobile devices has helped keep response times short, but the slowness of touch-screen typing makes personal notes more difficult)."

"The Patron Saint of Livestock" was picked up after approximately 18 rejections and four rewrites by *Cosmic Roots & Eldritch Shores*.

∼

Submit here:
https://www.diabolicalplots.com/guidelines/

7
ON SPEC

cience Fiction

Managing Editor: Diane Walton
   Pay: $100 for under 1,000 word
   Sliding scale up to $200
   Word range: up to 6,000
   Simultaneous submissions? Yes
   Ezine and Print - Based out of Canada

On Spec publishes innovative poetry and short stories. They call themselves:

 The Canadian Magazine of the Fantastic"

The editors ask for character-driven pieces with high stakes that keep readers turning the pages.

From the website:

"Our little quarterly journal, On Spec adheres to a strong mandate that has served us well over the years. We discover and showcase quality works by predominantly Canadian writers and artists, in the genre we call "Fantastic" literature. We foster the growth of emerging writers in this genre, by offering support and direction through constructive criticism, education, mentoring, and manuscript development. We try to publish as many new writers as possible, alongside works by established writers, and we also endeavour to support these writings with innovative cover art for every mind-bending and emotion-provoking issue!"

Here are some more hints for selling to this market:

- Watch out for flags that predict the ending of the story before we get to it.
- Don't send us a HAITE story. That's our acronym for "Here's An Idea: The End".
- Watch out for surprise Twist endings, especially if you have hidden a key piece of information from the Reader until the deus ex machina ending happens. The same applies to "one joke" or "Shaggy dog" endings.
- Make sure your story gives the reader a credible reason to willingly suspend their disbelief, and always make the ending of your story believable. The last thing we want to see is "It was all a dream", or "we're all living inside a snow globe", or "this was all VR".
- Stay away from really awful protagonists. Remember the point above where we want the reader to be engaged with the protagonist and really care about the outcome."

I've sent two stories to this market and one rejection letter contained some helpful hints:

"We are sorry to inform you that your Work entitled Quiver does not meet our needs. Thank you for giving us an opportunity to read it. The editors may have included some comments on your work which may be useful. Comments can be seen below. Keep in mind this is only the opinion of one magazine. We wish you the best in your future writing career, and hope to see more of your work. Please do not reply to this email notice.
First, two comments: Look up the verbs "to lie" and "to lay," and next, please set up your manuscript so that there is not an extra space between paragraphs. Thank you. This is an interesting premise but the execution needs work.

> The twist that Seth was not the killer was a nice device and worked very well, sending the story in an unexpected direction.

However, there were numerous grammatical and punctuation errors, along with awkward phrasing that detracted from the story."

This was a very valuable rejection letter for me. I didn't understand that the standard word document formatting comes with extra spaces after the last period before you make a new paragraph. Most editors hate that. (You can go into paragraph settings in Word and change this.)
A good reminder; make sure all your stories are well-edited before you send them in.
"Quiver" is in the process of being rewritten and turned into a paranormal romance novella. It features the same characters (Seth the leech man and Jill the cop) as "Shafted".

ANGELIQUE FAWNS

Submit here:
https://onspecmag.wpcomstaging.com/submissions/

8
STRANGE HORIZONS

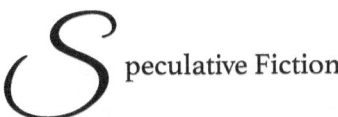peculative Fiction

Editor-in-chief: Vanessa Rose Phin
   Pay: 10 cents per word
   Word range: up to 5,000
   Simultaneous submissions? No
   Reprints? No
   Ezine and Podcast

Strange Horizons defines itself as a weekly magazine of and about speculative fiction. Launched in September 2000, it is a SWFA-qualifying market. The staff volunteering on this magazine come from all over the world including Sri Lanka, India, Brazil, Canada, China, and the USA.

From the website:

"We publish fiction, poetry, reviews, essays, interviews, round-table discussions, and art.

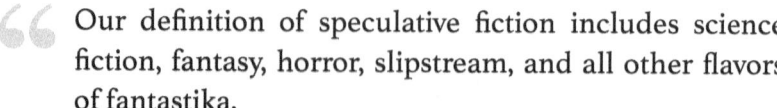Our definition of speculative fiction includes science fiction, fantasy, horror, slipstream, and all other flavors of fantastika.

Work published in Strange Horizons has been shortlisted for or won Hugo, Nebula, Rhysling, Theodore Sturgeon, James Tiptree Jr., and World Fantasy Awards.
Speculative fiction has a vibrant and radical tradition of stories that can make us think, can critique society, and can show us how it could be otherwise, for better or worse. We aim to be part of that tradition, and to update it: in the twenty-first century, speculative fiction must be a global, inclusive literature. We want to showcase work that challenges us and delights us, by new and established writers from diverse backgrounds and with diverse concerns."

They specify what kind of fiction they are looking for:

- Fiction from or about diverse perspectives and traditionally under-represented groups, settings, and cultures, written from a non-exoticizing and well-researched position.
- Unusual yet readable styles and inventive structures and narratives.
- Stories that address political issues in complex and nuanced ways, resisting oversimplification.
- Hypertext fiction, interactive fiction, and other stories that explore and exploit the forms available to us. If you have a work of this type that you think might be a good fit for Strange Horizons, please query us to discuss how to submit it."

The Guide of All Guides

The magazine, editors, stories, authors, and even the website, have been nominated for numerous awards and accolades. A writing credit from here is a feather in any speculative fiction creator's cap.

Strange Horizons has a "window" to submit your stories every week between Monday 1600 UTC and Tuesday 1600 UTC every month except during the month of December.

I've had two rejections from this market, and received standard letters:

"Thank you for submitting "Farmyard Follies" to Strange Horizons, and apologies for the delay in responding! We appreciate the chance to read your work but unfortunately this piece didn't quite work for us. We wish you the best in placing it elsewhere. We appreciate your interest in our magazine."

"Farmyard Follies" was self-published after 17 rejections and three rewrites. You can read this story and learn about its journey in *The Story Behind The Stories*.

I received the exact same letter for my story "Shafted". It took just over a month to get my responses. "Shafted" received nine rejections before I decided to attempt my first novella.

Submit here:
http://strangehorizons.com/submit/fiction-submission-guidelines/

9
ANALOG SCIENCE FICTION AND FACT

 cience Fiction

Editor: Trevor Quachi
  Pay: 8-10 cents per word
  Word range: up to 20,000
  Simultaneous submissions? No
  Reprints? No
  Ezine and Print - Based out of US

This is another founding magazine and big player in the science fiction world owned by Dell Magazines. *Analog Science Fiction and Fact Magazine* was originally published as *Astounding Stories of Science Fiction* when it launched in 1930.

Analog was where Anne McCaffrey's dragons first took flight! There were three issues from 1967 and 1968 which have the first three novellas in McCaffrey's Dragonriders of Pern series.

> Frank Herbert's sprawling epic *Dune* also originally appeared in *Analog*. After being serialized in the magazine, *Dune* was rejected 23 times before it was eventually picked up by Chilton Books. *Dune* has been called the best-selling science fiction novel of all time.

For our younger readers, Orson Scott Card's *Ender's Game* had its genesis in *Analog*.

Editor Trevor Quachri says:

"Analog/Astounding is often considered the magazine where science fiction grew up. When Editor John W. Campbell took over in 1938, he brought to Astounding an unprecedented insistence on placing equal emphasis on both words of "science fiction." No longer satisfied with gadgetry and action per se, Campbell demanded that his writers try to think out how science and technology might really develop in the future – and, most importantly, how those changes would affect the lives of human beings. The new sophistication soon made Astounding the undisputed leader in the field, and Campbell began to think the old title was too "sensational" to reflect what the magazine was actually doing. He chose "Analog" in part because he thought of each story as an "analog simulation" of a possible future, and in part because of the close analogy he saw between the imagined science in the stories he was publishing and the real science being done in laboratories around the world.

> Real science and technology have always been important in Analog, not only as the foundation of its fiction, but as the subject of articles about real research with big implications for the future.

One story published during World War II described an atomic bomb so accurately – before Hiroshima – that FBI agents visited John Campbell to find out where the leak was. (There was no leak – just attentive, forward-thinking writers!)"

For both my submissions, I received a standard rejection:

"Thank you very much for letting me see "The Corp." I'm sorry it didn't strike me as quite suitable to our present needs."

"The Corp" is still being worked on and has grown from a short story to a novella.
If you want to submit your fiction here, take note:

"We publish science fiction stories in which some aspect of future science or technology is so integral to the plot that, if that aspect were removed, the story would collapse.

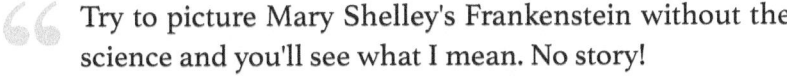
Try to picture Mary Shelley's Frankenstein without the science and you'll see what I mean. No story!

The science can be physical, sociological, psychological. The technology can be anything from electronic engineering to biogenetic engineering. But the stories must be strong and realistic, with believable people (who needn't be human) doing believable things–no matter how fantastic the background might be."

Submit here:
https://www.analogsf.com/contact-us/writers-guidelines/

10
AMAZING STORIES

*S*cience Fiction

Managing Editor: Ira Nayman
   Pay: 8 cents per word
   Word range: 1,000 -10,000
   Reprints? No
   Simultaneous submissions? No
   Print and Ezine - Based out of US

Amazing Stories has been around for a long time.

In fact, it credits itself as the very first science fiction magazine started in 1926 by Hugo Gernsback.

Stephen King talks about receiving rejections from this publication at the beginning of his career.

The website chronicles what *Amazing Stories* has done lately:

> The field of science fiction (or scientifiction as Gernsback originally called it) has changed substantially in the ninety years since Amazing Stories was first published.

For one thing, science has progressed substantially, giving us men on the moon, a map of the human genome, virtual reality, the Internet of things, and real robots and artificial intelligence; never before have science fiction writers had so many toys to play with, and new ones seem to be appearing every day. For another thing, science fiction readers are more sophisticated than they were an almost century ago; they've been there and done that with the formulae of the genre, and they're looking for what's next. Amazing Stories hopes to be what's next."

Amazing Stories has changed its format and is now putting together special theme issues. The first two themes are "Home Sweet Solar System" and "Everything Computes." However, you can still submit stories even if they don't conform to a theme.

The guidelines say:

"Amazing Stories is looking for short stories that are fresh and new. We want to be surprised. We want to be delighted. We want your stories to be amazing.

> It's not enough to be technically proficient and have a sort of, somewhat semi-original idea; we want to be dazzled by your original style and substance.

Remember when science fiction was optimistic, when the future was something to be embraced as a bold adventure instead of a place of dystopias, seemingly endless wars and mutant monstrosities to be feared? Amazing Stories will not shy away from stories that explore the negative impacts of technologies on individuals and society, but we have a strong preference for stories that take a bright view of human ingenuity and the possible futures we can make with it.

> Have you ever read a short story or novel and thought to yourself, "I want to take part in making that future a reality?"

That is what we would like to see.
We intend to have a balance of relatively known and relatively new writers. Don't be reluctant to submit stories just because you aren't a famous writer – if you have an original idea and style, submitting to Amazing Stories could be your first step to becoming one.
We are happy to consider stories with a strong point of view, especially in light of the fact that one of the strengths of science fiction is its exploration of how science and technology can change interpersonal relationships and politics. However, we do not want stories that are basically political screeds or other kinds of preaching. The point of view needs to arise naturally out of the workings of the plot and the interactions of the characters."

I have received standard rejections in good time from *Amazing*:

"Thank you for submitting your story "The Attack of the Leech People" to Amazing Stories. Unfortunately, it is not what we are looking for at this time. Best of luck with your future writing."

"The Attack of the Leech People" has been rejected 3 times. It stars my leech man Seth, (also in "Quiver" and "Shafted") and is being worked into a paranormal romance novella.

Submit here:
   https://submission.amazingstoriesmag.com/

11

APEX MAGAZINE

ark Fantastical Fiction

Editor: Jason Sizemore
   Pay: 8 cents per word
   Word range: up to 7,500
   Simultaneous submissions? No
   Reprints? No
   Ezine - Based out of US

Apex Magazine focuses on dark and spectacular science fiction, fantasy and horror. Publishing bi-monthly, it used to be called *Apex Digest* and has been nominated for several awards. It went on hiatus for a while, but is back in business and accepting submissions.

Apex Magazine has published work by Neil Gaiman, Maurice Broaddus and Cherie Priest.

From the website:

"Apex Magazine is an online zine of fantastical fiction.

> We publish short stories filled with marrow and passion, works that are twisted, strange, and beautiful.

Creations where secret places and dreams are put on display. We publish in two forms: an every-other-month eBook issue and a gradual release of an entire issue online over a two-month period. Along with the genre short fiction, there are interviews with authors and nonfiction essays about current issues. Additionally, we produce a monthly podcast of narrated original short fiction."

I've sent four stories to them and they get back with a rejection in good time. Here is how my rejections have looked for all four (sub in a different story name):

"Thank you for submitting "Invasive Species" to Apex Magazine. We appreciate the chance to read it. Unfortunately, the story does not meet our needs at this time. We're going to pass. I wish you the best of luck finding a home for "Invasive Species" and I hope to read something new from you soon."

"Invasive Species" is the very first fiction story I ever wrote and it took me three years to find it a home. It's finally been accepted by a pro-market.

～

Submit here:
https://apex-magazine.com/submission-guidelines/

12

BENEATH CEASELESS SKIES

*L*iterary Adventure Fantasy

Editor: Scott H. Andrews
　Pay: 8 cents per word
　Word range: under 15,000 words
　Simultaneous submissions? Yes
　Reprints? No
　Ezine and Podcast - Based out of US

Beneath Ceaseless Skies has been bringing fantasy adventure stories from pre-tech worlds to readers since October, 2008. This is another SFWA-qualifying magazine with absolutely breathtaking cover art and award-winning short stories.

　From the website:

"We love traditional adventure fantasy, but we also love how the influence of literary writing on fantasy short fiction has expanded the genre, encouraging writers to use literary devices such as tight points-of-view and discontinuous narratives; to feature conflicts that are internal as well as external. We want stories that combine the best of both these styles—set in vivid fantasy or historical paranormal worlds but written with all the flair and impact of modern literary-influenced fantasy."

To help understand what kind of world they're looking for; here is how they describe secondary-world settings:

"We want stories set in what Tolkien called a "secondary world": some other world that is different from our own primary world in some way. It could be different in terms of zoology (non-human creatures), ecology (climate), or physical laws (the presence of magic).
It could be set on Earth but an Earth different from our modern-day primary world in terms of time (the pre-modern historical past of our real-world Earth) or history (alternate history from our Earth's history).

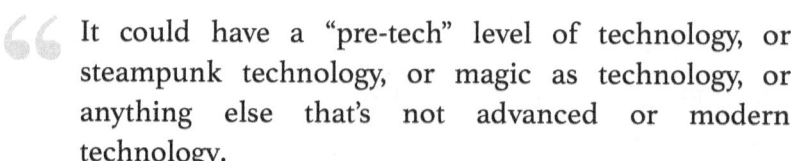

It could have a "pre-tech" level of technology, or steampunk technology, or magic as technology, or anything else that's not advanced or modern technology.

However, the setting should contain some element that is in some way fantastical, and the qualities of the setting should have some bearing on the rest of the story.
We are NOT interested in urban fantasy or other types of stories set in our modern, contemporary "real world," even if they contain fantasy elements, or in stories that move between the real world and a fantasy world."

I've submitted two stories here, but I haven't managed to hit the kind of tale they are looking for. There is a very specific kind of world this publication features. Both my rejections read:

> "Thanks very much for sending this story to Beneath Ceaseless Skies. Unfortunately, it's not quite right for me. We publish fantasy set in pre-tech worlds; this setting to me felt too modern for us. We appreciate your interest in our magazine. Please feel free to submit other work in the future."

I find they do get back to you quite quickly. Both my rejections rolled in the day after I submitted, and the website promises:

> All our rejection letters are personalized, which many new and neo-pro writers tell us they find helpful in revising their stories to submit elsewhere and in developing their writing in general."

Submit here:
http://www.beneath-ceaseless-skies.com/submissions/

13

MYSTERION

hristian Speculative Fiction

Editor: Donald S. Crankshaw
   Editor: Kristin Janz
   Pay: 8 cents per word
   Word range: up to 9,000
   Simultaneous submissions? No
   Reprints? Yes, 4 cents per word

Mysterion is an ezine focusing on the mysteries of the Christian faith and has been publishing since 2008. The husband-and-wife team running it also produce beautiful paperback anthologies featuring stories from the online magazine. They are looking for speculative fiction with Christian characters, themes or cosmology.

Authors don't have to be Christian to submit, and the editors prefer fiction that challenges rather than confirms their beliefs.

The website explains:

"The Christian faith is filled with mystery, from the Trinity and the Incarnation to the smaller mysteries found in some of the strange and unexplained passages of the Bible: Behemoth and Leviathan, nephilim and seraphim, heroes and giants and more. There is no reason for fiction engaging with Christianity to be more tidy and theologically precise than the faith itself."

I've submitted two stories to the market, and Donald S. Crankshaw gave me some helpful advice in one of his rejection letters.

"Thank you for submitting "Linked Lives" to Mysterion. We appreciate having the chance to read it. Unfortunately, we have decided not to accept it for publication.

> I thought the world was interesting and the story was well-written, but while it was a straightforward projection from current trends, it was too much of a straight-line projection, without the twists and turns that you usually find in real history.

For example, no matter how luxurious a society is, there are always people who opt out.
Also, I found the idea of cellphones causing cancer in people's heads less believable than it would have been in the early 2000s. While modern smartphones are heavily used, they don't spend much time near people's heads, and they usually come with headsets."

I took his notes into consideration, rewrote and renamed the story as "A Time to Forget" and sold it to *Pulp Modern: Tech Noir*.
You can read about that tale's journey in *The Story Behind The Stories*.

Submit here:
https://mysterion.moksha.io/publication/mysterion

14

FANTASY MAGAZINE

antasy & Dark Fantasy

Editor-in-Chief: Arley Sorg
   Pay: 8 cents per word
   Word range: 1,500-7,500
   Simultaneous submissions? No
   Reprints? No
   Ezine and Print - Based out of US

Fantasy Magazine is part of the powerhouse speculative publishing family of Adamant Press; owned and operated by John Joesph Adams and Christie Yant. Adams has won the Hugo Award twice and is the bestselling editor of more than 30 anthologies.

Fantasy Magazine, *Lightspeed Magazine* and *Nightmare Magazine* are all SFWA-qualified, critically-acclaimed and sought-after writing credits for authors.

From the website:

"Fantasy Magazine is a digital magazine focusing exclusively on the fantasy genre. In its pages, you will find all types of fantasy—dark fantasy, contemporary urban tales, surrealism, magical realism, science fantasy, high fantasy, folktales...and anything and everything in between.

> Fantasy is entertainment for the intelligent genre reader—we publish stories of the fantastic that make us think, and tell us what it is to be human."

Fantasy Magazine is open to submissions the first week of every month (1st-7th), and they only accept anonymous submissions, so double check your manuscript before sending it in through the Moksha system.

I've sent three stories their way. So far, they have responded to my submissions fairly quickly and have a short rejection letter that I received for all.

"Thank you for submitting "The Museum of The Lost People," but it didn't quite work for us. We hope you are able to place this one elsewhere."

"The Museum of the Lost People", a magical realism short, is still looking for a home.

∼

Submit here:
https://adamant.moksha.io/publication/fantasy/guidelines

15
NIGHTMARE MAGAZINE

*H*orror & Dark Fantasy

Editor: Wendy N. Wagnor
　Pay: 8 cents per word
　Word range: 1500-7500
　Simultaneous submissions? No
　Reprints? No
　Ezine and Print- Based out of US

Nightmare Magazine is the darker imprint of Adamant Press; owned and operated by John Joesph Adams. *Fantasy Magazine, Lightspeed Magazine* and *Nightmare Magazine* are all critically-acclaimed and sought-after writing credits for authors.

From the website:

"Nightmare is a horror and dark fantasy magazine.

In Nightmare's pages, you will find all kinds of horror fiction, from zombie stories and haunted house tales, to visceral psychological horror…

When you read Nightmare, it is our hope that you'll see where horror comes from, where it is now, and where it's going."

The guidelines state that, "no subject should be considered off-limits."
They also offer *The Horror Lab*:

"'The Horror Lab' is where Nightmare puts a spotlight on experimental horror. It's a place to explore the boundaries of form, trope, and genre—a playground for writers and readers alike. We're looking for poetry (all styles and forms, but due to the limitations of eBooks generally and Kindle Periodicals specifically our typographical options are limited), flash fiction, and creative non-fiction. (And yes, dark fantasy is fine!)"

I've had one story rejected by *Nightmare*.
Here is my letter:

"Thanks for submitting "The Museum of the Lost People," but I'm going to pass on it. It didn't quite work for me, I'm afraid. Best of luck to you placing this one elsewhere, and thanks again for sending it my way."

"The Museum of the Lost People" is making the rounds being rejected by most of the top markets.
If you have a story rejected by *Nightmare*, they do not want you to resubmit it to *Lightspeed*, but you can try *Fantasy*.

Submit here:
https://adamant.moksha.io/publication/nightmare/guidelines

16

LIGHTSPEED MAGAZINE

cience Fiction & Fantasy

Publisher/Editor: John Joseph Adams
　Pay: 8 cents per word
　Word range: 1,500-10,000
　Simultaneous submissions? No
　Reprints? Yes, 2 cents a word
　Ezine and Print- Based out of US

Lightspeed Magazine is the most well-known and critically acclaimed sister publication of Adamant Press; owned and operated by John Joesph Adams.
　From the website:

"Lightspeed is a digital science fiction and fantasy magazine. In its pages, you will find science fiction: from near-future, sociological soft SF, to far-future, star-spanning hard SF—and fantasy: from epic fantasy, sword-and-sorcery, and contemporary urban tales, to magical realism, science-fantasy, and folktales."

> Many famous authors have had stories in Lightspeed, including Stephen King, George R.R. Martin, Ursula K. Le Guin, Neil Gaiman, N.K. Jemisin, Ted Chiang, and Ken Liu.

I haven't submitted a story to *Lightspeed* yet because I've never hit the submission window when it is open.

Submit here:
https://adamant.moksha.io/publication/lightspeed/guidelines

17

DEEP MAGIC

lean Fantasy & Science Fiction

Founder: Brendon Taylor
 Pay: 8 cents per word (first 7,499)
 Word range: 1,000 - 40,000
 Simultaneous submissions? No
 Reprints? Yes, 2 cents per word
 Ezine & Print- Based out of US

Deep Magic is looking for stories that don't rely on sex, swearing or violence.

From the website:

> The name Deep Magic pays homage to C.S. Lewis's The Chronicles of Narnia.

From June 2002 to June of 2006, Deep Magic was a monthly e-zine operated by a nonprofit organization founded by three friends who had a mutual love of SFF and a desire to promote clean writing within those genres. Deep Magic is now a quarterly publication that pays professional rates for SFF short fiction, relaunched by the same three friends, with help of other industry professionals who join in Deep Magic's mission to create a safe place for minds to wander.

We will consider stories within any sub-genre (epic, paranormal, steampunk, etc.).

> The best way to get our attention with your submissions is to create great tension in your story."

On average I've had to wait two months to get a reply to my submissions. I've received three rejections from this market and here is one of my letters:

"Thank you for your submission to Deep Magic. We know it can be stressful waiting for a response and we strive to be as prompt as we can. We are going to pass on your submission, The Pandemic Pet, although we do appreciate you considering us. Writing is very subjective and just because we didn't select this piece doesn't mean others won't. It just wasn't the right fit for us. Thank you again for submitting your work to Deep Magic. You are always more than welcome to submit something else in the future so long as it meets our guidelines."

I've rewritten "The Pandemic Pet" as "The Museum of the Lost People" and even with a title change, I'm still getting plenty of rejections (many from the publications in this guide.) I'm looking for the next market to submit it to.

Submit here:
https://deepmagic.co/submissions/#

18

ELLERY QUEEN MYSTERY MAGAZINE

*M*ystery

Editor: Janet Hutchings
 Pay: 5-8 cents per word
 Word range: 250-12,000
 Short novels up to 20,000
 Simultaneous submissions? No
 Print - Based out of US

Ellery Queen Mystery Magazine (EQMM) has been around since 1941 and has been cited as "the finest periodical of its kind" by The Readers Encyclopedia of American Literature. They pay professional rates and have short stories from famous authors in many editions.

Writers like William Faulkner, Agatha Christie, Ian

> Rankin, Val McDermid, Ruth Rendell and Peter
> Robinson have been featured.

It is a part of the Dell Magazine family along with *Alfred Hitchcock Mystery Magazine.*

Their website proclaims they are the "winner of more than 100 major awards, including 22 Edgars from the Mystery Writers of America, *EQMM* is the most celebrated mystery and crime-fiction publication in the world."

I've been reading *Ellery Queen Mystery Magazine* since the age of 9 years old and enjoy the short twisty tales. I was fortunate to have one of my first sales here. You can learn more about it in my full-length short story anthology (plus publisher insights) *The Story Behind The Stories.* "Three Calendars" was selected to be featured in the Department of First Stories.

The writer's guidelines state:

"We publish every kind of mystery short story: the psychological suspense tale, the deductive puzzle, the private eye case—the gamut of crime and detection from the realistic (including the policeman's lot and stories of police procedure) to the more imaginative (including "locked rooms" and "impossible crimes").

> We need hard-boiled stories as well as "cozies," but we are not interested in explicit sex or violence.

We do not want true detective or crime stories. With the exception of a regular book review column and a mystery crossword, EQMM publishes only fiction.

> We are especially happy to review first stories by authors who have never before published fiction professionally.

First-story submissions should be addressed to EQMM's Department of First Stories."

The acceptance was exciting, but I haven't managed to sell them another tale yet. I've sent two more Janet Hutching's way. Here is my last rejection letter:

"Thanks for letting us see "Quiver (revision)." I like your writing, but I can't quite see this story as something for EQMM. I hope you will soon sell it elsewhere. We'll look forward to seeing more of your work."

"Quiver" is currently being turned into a paranormal romance novel with some mystery elements. Not every market is looking for a story featuring a leech man with a heart of gold.

Submit Here:
http://eqmm.magazinesubmissions.com

19

ALFRED HITCHCOCK MYSTERY MAGAZINE

Mystery

Editor: Linda Landrigan
Pay: 5-8 cents per word
Word range: up to 12,000
Simultaneous submissions? No
Reprints? No
Print - Based out of US

Alfred Hitchcock Mystery Magazine publishes mystery, crime, and suspense short stories.

Debuting in 1956, you could find stories from writers such as Donald Westlake, Ed McBain, and Hillary Waugh.

The editor Linda Landrigan advises:

Great stories of any genre are rooted in characters — well-drawn, individual, and credibly motivated.

Interesting characters responding to the extraordinary pressures of crime — this is what I like to read and to publish, and I hope you like that too."

The guidelines say:

"Finding new authors is a great pleasure for all of us here, and we look forward to reading the fiction you send us. Since we do read all submissions, there is no need to query first; please send the entire story. You don't need an agent. Because this is a mystery magazine, the stories we buy must fall into that genre in some sense or another. We are interested in nearly every kind of mystery: stories of detection of the classic kind, police procedurals, private eye tales, suspense, courtroom dramas, stories of espionage, and so on.

 We ask only that the story be about a crime (or the threat or fear of one).

We sometimes accept ghost stories or supernatural tales, but those also should involve a crime."

I've had two rejections here, and they both took almost a year to get back to me.
Here is my letter:

"Thank you very much for letting us see "The Patron Saint of Livestock." We appreciate your taking the time to send it in for our consideration. Although it does not suit the needs of the magazine at this time, we wish you luck with placing it elsewhere. Please excuse this form letter. The volume of work has unfortunately made it impossible for us to respond to each submission individually, much as we'd like to do so."

"The Patron Saint of Livestock" does have a mystery with a missing ring in the plot, but is primarily a dark speculative story and has been picked up by *Cosmic Roots & Eldritch Shores*.

Submit here:

https://www.alfredhitchcockmysterymagazine.com/contact-us/writers-guidelines/

20

THE RECKONING

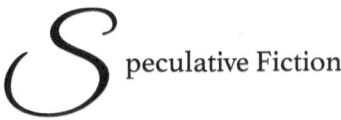peculative Fiction

Editor: Andrew Kozma
    Pay: 8 cents per word
    Word range: 0 - 20,000
    Simultaneous submissions? Yes
    Reprints? Query first
    eBook and Print - Based out of US

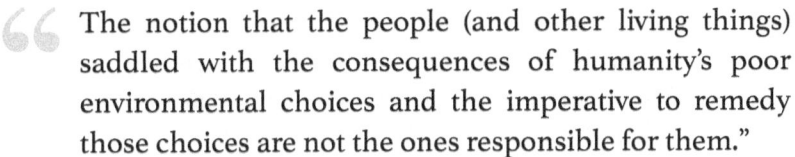

Reckoning Magazine is a nonprofit annual journal that focuses on environmental justice. They define environmental justice as:

> The notion that the people (and other living things) saddled with the consequences of humanity's poor environmental choices and the imperative to remedy those choices are not the ones responsible for them."

The guidelines specify:

"Seeking speculative fiction, creative nonfiction, and poetry about environmental justice that addresses the intersection between social upheaval and environmental changes, from collapses to breakthroughs, and everything in between. People's large-scale relationships to the Earth produce formidable stories of devastation and resilience, which we welcome, but we also welcome those moments of intimacy, of quiet revolution, of deciding that changing the world means understanding and fighting for one's place in it.

> We're especially interested in work that demolishes or subverts binaries; that engages all the senses and emotions; and deals in hope, complexity, and complicity.

Fiction that shatters, stretches, or realigns mainstream Western ideas about relationships between individual humans, humans as a whole, and all other members of our environment. We'd love to read something with the vibe of Leslie Marmon Silko, Linda Hogan, N.K. Jemisin, or something brand-new.

> Send us your solarpunk, your biopunk, your hopepunk, and all things of multiple genres.

Nonfiction stories of environmental racism, of mental health intertwined with climate justice, of reckoning with systemic inequities during natural disasters, be they incisive or philosophical, bleak or hopeful, private or macrocosmic.
Poetry that deals with the questions of: how does social justice impact the manifestations, understanding and assimilation of environmental justice? How are attitudes toward preservation influenced—or complicated by—cultural roots? How have

civil rights exposed or strengthened breaches in the makeup of activism?"

Something quite wonderful about this market is the personalized rejections I've received for every story. Here are three of mine:

"Thank you very much for submitting, but I'm sorry to say I can't accept "Camp Blue Marble" for Reckoning. While it did address the theme of climate change, I felt it was a pretext for the plot rather than a central element (it could have been replaced by any other problem big enough to warrant the creation of a protected dome for children of the elite). I also felt that the short story format did not allow the setting to be developed to its full potential."

This story was reworked and purchased by The Great Void Publishing for their anthology *Unreal*. Read more about it in *The Publishers Behind The Pages*.
Another rejection:

"Thank you very much for submitting "Invasive Species" to Reckoning, but unfortunately it isn't what we're looking for right now.

The concept, while clever, is somewhat overdone -- we see a lot of aliens-as-invasives go by.

Best of luck in placing this elsewhere."

"Invasive Species" found a home with *DreamForge Anvil*.
And finally:

"Thank you very much for submitting, but I'm sorry to say I can't accept "The Patron Saint of Livestock" for Reckoning. In part, I felt the story jumped too quickly between events without ever really having continuity between them, and I wanted more depth to the characterization."

"The Patron Saint of Livestock" is with *Cosmic Roots & Eldritch Shores.*

∼

Submit here:
https://reckoning.press/submit/

21

COSSMASS INFINITIES

cience Fiction & Fantasy

Editor: Paul Campbell
 Pay: 8c per word
 Word range: 2,000-10,000
 Simultaneous submissions? Yes
 Reprints? No
 eBook and print- Based out of Scotland

Cossmass Infinites is published three times a year and buys original science fiction and fantasy short stories. It is a SFWA-qualified market, and you can read some of the stories for free on the website. This project is run by Paul Campbell and he explains on the website:

> There is no company behind Cossmass Infinities. There is just me, Paul Campbell, currently paying for

everything out of my own pocket. Each issue costs around $3300 produce."

Campbell explains where the inspiration for the name *Cossmass Infinities* comes from:

"Once, many, many years ago, I was running a Role Playing Game at some University in Edinburgh one Sunday afternoon. It was a reality hopping adventure initially inspired by WAXWORK II: LOST IN TIME. One of the players asked me what the name of the setting was. I'd never actually thought of what to call it before. What was the plural of Cosmos? 'Cosmoses' or 'comoi'? Both would have been great, even correct. I didn't know either at the time. Under pressure to give a confident answer to my players, I mashed Cosmos and 'mass' (large in number), and said "The Cossmass"."
Infinities is simply a plural form of Infinity. Okay, this one was a bit obvious.
So, Cossmass Infinities is "a multiple infinite number of many Cosmoses". More than a few possibilities, then."

He sent me a standard rejection to the one story I sent him. The turnaround was less than two months to hear back about my paranormal short "Quiver.":

"Unfortunately, we are choosing not to use this story. Please feel free to submit another story that you would like us to consider for publication when we are next open for submissions."

"Quiver" is my take on the vampire story, but instead of being a sexy creature of the night, Seth is a fat, bald farmer who sucks blood because he is a leech man. I'm creating a novella with combining three of my unsold stories starring Seth.

Submit here:
https://www.cossmass.com/submit/

22

DREAMFORGE ANVIL

antasy & Science Fiction

Editor: Scot Noel
   Pay: 6 cents per word
   Word range: prefers under 4,500
   Simultaneous submissions? Yes
   Reprints? Yes 4-5 cents per word
   Print and Ezine - Based out of the US

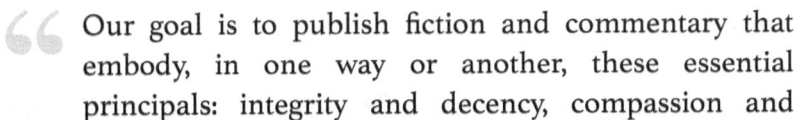

DreamForge is a fantasy and science fiction magazine that looks for positive stories. The website says:

> Our goal is to publish fiction and commentary that embody, in one way or another, these essential principals: integrity and decency, compassion and

creativity, intelligence and inventiveness, the rule of law and liberty under the law, and the dignity of the individual."

I really like this market. Their webpage provides an article helping you understand why they didn't buy your story. I've submitted five stories to this market which were rejected. They allow you to request feedback when you submit your piece. I am so glad I requested feedback, because I took Scot Noel's advice and completely rewrote "The Patron Saint of Livestock." When I resubmitted it to *Cosmic Roots & Eldritch Shores,* it was picked up dependent on revisions.

Here is the feedback I received from Noel:

"Angelique, you submitted "The Patron Saint of Livestock". Your writing shows promise in its command of language and pacing. For us, the biggest problem was that you are literally "telling" a story, as in recounting incidents and providing authorial exposition.

> For our needs, we're looking for works which show rather than tell, ones that provide a hook and then engage the reader in a buildup of tension through to the climax of the story.

Keep in mind I also just heard from another hopeful contributor that the story we sent back just sold to another magazine. That doesn't make us right or them wrong - it just means the author kept submitting and found a better fit for that particular work.
We wish you all the best and hope you find a good home for your story too."

I also submitted "Camp Napanoo" (originally called "Camp Blue Marble") to *DreamForge* requesting feedback.

"Thank you for your patience while we reviewed your story "Camp Blue Marble," unfortunately, we're going to pass this time. While we appreciated your story, we felt it wasn't right for us. Our team noted a few things that were problematic for us. They were:

> The dialogue is quite stilted and the character motivations and reactions feel contrived. Would be improved with less telling and more showing.

Some vague and cliched descriptions. We look forward to seeing work from you again in the future, and we wish you luck with submitting this story to other venues (it may be fine as is for another editor). As we publish more stories and unlock more of them for registered users and visitors, please do read us and you'll get a better sense of what seems to catch our fancy."

I used those notes, changed the name from "Camp Blue Marble" to "Camp Napanoo" and it was picked up by an anthology called *Unreal*, published by The Great Void. You can read about "Camp Napanoo's" journey in *The Publishers Behind The Pages*.

In 2021, DreamForge is changing direction a bit in response to COVID-19 related challenges. You can read more here:

The New Direction

Scot Noel is using "Invasive Species" for this new initiative.

∼

Submit your stories here:

https://dreamforgemagazine.com/call-for-submissions/

23

COSMIC ROOTS & ELDRITCH SHORES

cience Fiction & Fantasy

Editor: Fran Eisemann
  Pay: 6 cents per word
  Word range: 1,000-upwards.
  Simultaneous submissions? No
  Reprints? Yes, 2 cents per word
  Ezine – Based out of the US

Cosmic Roots & Eldritch Shores is one of my favorite places to submit stories. They have been publishing sublime shorts since New Year's Eve 2015-2016.

From their website:

Our Mission... is to explore our universe and its wild eldritch shores, to seek out new writers and story forms, to boldly go through time, mind, and the cosmos.

Here are our stories and art - classic and new, imagination and fact, serious and humorous - from around the world and throughout time, our own special brew and broad-spectrum formulation for young and old, of words, artwork, graphic novels, videos, animation, and podcasts in...

- Science Fiction - hard as steel, soft as velvet, electrifying as lightning, solid as gold, insubstantial as interstellar near-vacuum; from space opera, steampunk, AU, cyber, to humorous.
- Fantasy - AU, epic, historical, urban, magical realism, steampunk.
- Myths, legends, fairy tales - ancient original versions and present-day reworking, from all times and parts of the world.
- Eldritch - otherworldly encounters, beyond the pale, ghostly, eerie, uncanny, mysteries of the night and the mind, slipping between the spaces."

They accept submissions on the first and second day of every month, and created The Kepler Award to:

 Recognize and encourage writers of excellent science fiction and fantasy stories that creatively extrapolate on known science in constructive and exciting ways."

Writers cannot get better without feedback, and *Cosmic Roots & Eldritch Shores* allows you to request feedback on your submission. I have had ten rejections from this market.

I submitted a story about singing chickens called "Farmyard Follies":

The Guide of All Guides

"Hi Angelique. Thanks for your submission. It was cute (and I also have chickens and a rooster) but the story won't quite work for us.
P.S. -- Roosters can be great if you understand their motivations and work with them."

Here is another rejection for a story about Seth, a leech man, and his romance with Jill, a small-town cop:

"Hi, Angelique. Thank you for submitting "Quiver." Unfortunately, we are declining. Since you requested feedback, I am copying below my comments. Please bear in mind these comments are not meant for comprehensive (or diplomatic) critique.

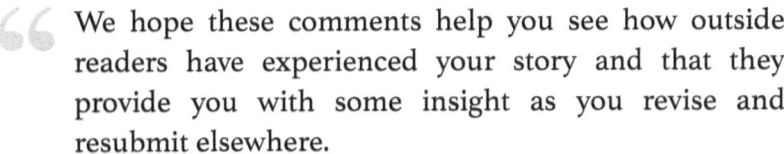

We hope these comments help you see how outside readers have experienced your story and that they provide you with some insight as you revise and resubmit elsewhere.

1) Bit of a slow start, with Jill's meandering appreciation of the local smells. A bit of a trim in the first couple or three paragraphs would strengthen the hook. Just enough to establish Jill's character and enough setting to orient readers to time and place. This sense of extraneous detail pervades the entire work. Streamlining will keep the momentum moving forward and improve the pacing, which feels a little slow.

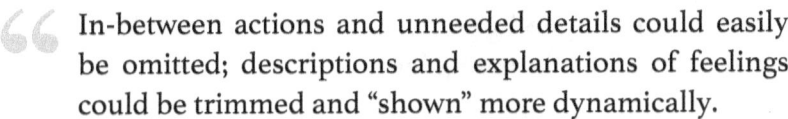

In-between actions and unneeded details could easily be omitted; descriptions and explanations of feelings could be trimmed and "shown" more dynamically.

The story starts to get a bit untenable when Jill meets Seth in the bar: The narrative and dialogue have a stilted, "written" effect (on-the-nose, move-the-plot-forward obviousness)

Then, it seems extremely unlikely that a) the owner of the local farm wouldn't be known about town (no mention is made of him being a recluse), or that b) Jill would blurt out crime scene information. And then, wow, this statement is a stretch: "Someone with my condition can only die from a sudden injection of salt. The most effective way to deliver the amount of sodium needed is with an arrow. The tip filled with salt." I mean, this is certainly ONE way to do it, but it's not the first one that would pop into anyone's mind. I also found the counterpoint, "Bullets don't work. Can't deliver enough salt" a bit outside the believable. These assertions make the key plot points feel like devices and conveniences rather than organic and necessary steps. Also, Jill shooting before the woman actually attacked and without any proof that she was the perpetrator of the earlier murders is presumptive and dangerous (= poor police work).

> Beyond these logic leaps and distractions, the story never really gains any tension.

This is for two key reasons: 1) The aforementioned extraneous material keeps the pacing. 2) Jill doesn't do anything particularly difficult in the story. Her discovery of the perpetrator's type (a leech-human hybrid on the loose) is handed to her when Seth seeks her out and reveals his condition. He also hands her the solution and the weapon to stop the killings. Moreover, finding the perp and stopping her is as simple as one night in a deer blind and a convenient, almost immediate appearance. Jill shoots from above and isn't challenged in the slightest. Easy for Jill = boring for readers.

> Whatever the problems in execution, I did enjoy the concept of a leech-human hybrid character.

If the logic leaps were addressed and the action made more dynamic and challenging, there might be some potential."

I am currently trying to turn "Quiver" into a paranormal romance novella.

Cosmic Roots & Eldritch Shores has accepted my story "A Patron Saint of Livestock", dependent upon revisions.

∼

Submit here:
https://cosmicrootsandeldritchshores.com/submissions/

24

THE DARK MAGAZINE

Horror & Dark Fantasy

Editor: Sean Wallace
  Pay: 6 cents per word
  Word range: 2,000-6,000
  Simultaneous submissions? No
  Reprints? No
  Ezine - Based out of US

The Dark Magazine sends out rejections fast and furiously. It's one of the reasons I like submitting to them. Instant results. They publish horror and dark fantasy.

> *Sean Wallace is the founder, publisher, and editor of The Dark, and has also edited for Clarkesworld and Fantasy Magazine.*

From the website:

"Don't be afraid to experiment or to deviate from the ordinary; be different—try us with fiction that may fall out of "regular" categories. However, it is also important to understand that despite the name,

 The Dark is not a market for graphic, violent horror."

I've had ten rejections from this magazine, and send them almost every story I write that has a shadowy feel. I haven't figured this market out yet and get the same letter each time:

"We have read your submission and unfortunately your story isn't quite what we're looking for right now. While we regretfully cannot provide detailed feedback due to the volume of submissions, we thank you for your interest in our magazine and hope you continue to consider us in the future."

Submit here:
https://www.thedarkmagazine.com/submission-guidelines/

25

ABYSS & APEX MAGAZINE

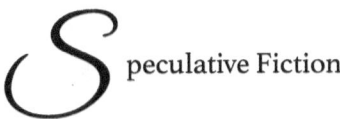peculative Fiction

Editor: Wendy S. Delmater
    Pay: 8c a word up to 1000 words
    Word range: up to 10,000
    Simultaneous submissions? No
    Reprints? No
    Ezine - Based out of US

Abyss & Apex is a Hugo-nominated magazine founded in 2003 and the title comes from a famous quote:

> *"And if you gaze long into the abyss, the abyss gazes also into you."*
>
> — FRIEDRICH NIETZSCHE

Abyss & Apex is not to be confused with *Apex Magazine*, also mentioned in this guide. *Apex Magazine* publishes darker stories and accepts horror.

From the website:

"Our mission is to publish the finest in speculative and imaginative fiction and poetry, with special attention to character-driven stories that examine the depths and heights of emotion and motivation from a broad variety of cultural and social perspectives. A&A wants to publish powerful stories with emotions that resonate in our minds and hearts long after a first reading, stories that make us want to read them again and again.

> We look for the unique: stories that stand out in a genre that pushes the envelope of unusual.

We take special delight in detailed world-building: we like slipstream, YA, hypertext fiction, dark fantasy, science fiction puzzle stories, magical realism, hard science fiction, soft science fiction, science fantasy, urban fantasy, military science fiction, ghost stories, space opera, cyberpunk, steampunk... there is very little we will not look at, although

> we have a severe allergy to zombies, elves, retold fairy tales, sports, westerns, vampires, and gratuitous sex and violence.

We have no subject/topic preference, beyond a requirement that the work have a speculative element. We are happy to read stories that don't quite seem to fit elsewhere.
We will consider dark speculative fiction, but we do not publish horror. We won't publish extremely graphic violent or sexual content or over-the-top gore either; we are turned off by gratuitous foul language. In other words, if the primary

purpose of a story is to scare us or make us queasy, we won't buy it."

I sent them "Invasive Species" (the seventh rewrite) and got a rejection the same day:

"Thank you for submitting your story to ABYSS & APEX. It was well received here, but after some thought we have decided not to accept it for publication. I hope you'll consider us again, and I wish you the best success in placing this story elsewhere."

The eighth rewrite finally found my alien invasion opus a home with *DreamForge Anvil*. The editor Scot Noel is helping me through a ninth revision.

Submit here:
https://www.abyssapexzine.com/submissions/

26

ZOOSCAPE

urry Fiction

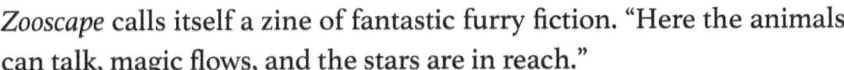

Editor-in-Chief: Mary E. Lowd
   Pay: 8c a word up to 1,000 words
   $80 flat rate for longer stories
   Word range: up to 10,000
   Reprints? $20
   Ezine - Based out of the US

Zooscape calls itself a zine of fantastic furry fiction. "Here the animals can talk, magic flows, and the stars are in reach."

> Mary E. Lowd is the editor, and her bio says "she lives in a crashed spaceship disguised as a house and hidden behind a rose garden, with an extensive menagerie of animals, some real and some imaginary."

I enjoy anthropomorphizing animals in my stories, and am obsessed with books like *Watership Down* and *Rats of NIMH*, so I like submitting to this market.

Their guidelines state:

"All stories must be furry. That means an anthropomorphic animal figure should be significantly featured in your story — it could be anthropomorphic in body or only intelligence. We'll consider any type of furry fiction from secret life of animals to fox in Starbucks.

> We love science-fiction with animal-like aliens and fantasy with talking dragons, unicorns, or witch familiars.

We are interested in underrepresented voices. If you have personal experience relevant to your story, feel free to mention it in your cover letter. For instance, if your story is about a space unicorn and you are a space unicorn (or a research biologist who studies space unicorns), let us know. We welcome and will be looking for diverse voices. We are not interested in stories that give voice to racist or sexist ideologies. And while we like unicorns and dragons, we find focusing on virginity, at best, tedious."

They get back to submissions in decent time. I've never had to wait more than a few weeks for my six rejections. Here is the standard letter:

"Thank you for submitting, "Planet Ten," to Zooscape. Unfortunately, it doesn't quite suit our needs. I wish you the best of luck with it elsewhere, and I hope you'll keep us in mind in the future."

"Planet Ten" still hasn't found a home, and it features AI animals planning to overthrow a future society.

I once also got a personalized note:

"Thank you for submitting, "Beware the Wog," to Zooscape.

> Unfortunately, while it's a delightfully creative piece, it doesn't quite suit our needs.

I wish you the best of luck with it elsewhere, and I hope you'll keep us in mind in the future."

"Beware the Wog" was retitled and rewritten as "Wyatt and the Whog" and sold to Mannison Press for their *Little Boy Lost* anthology. You can read about that story's journey in *The Publishers Behind The Pages*, another book in this series.

~

Submit here:
https://zooscape-zine.com/guidelines/

27

VISIONS

iterary Science Fiction

Publisher/Editor: Mathieu Triay
    Pay: 6 cents per word
    Word range: micro fiction - 3,000
    Simultaneous submissions? Yes
    Reprints? No
    Print and on-line - Based out of UK

Kudos to the design team for the *Visions* website. The stark color (white on black), and the use of empty space is dramatic and startling. There is a blurb on the home page which discusses the typography:

"We have put a lot of care in the design of the magazine to

create a great reading experience. As part of this effort, we revived and expanded a typeface specifically for our needs and it runs through the entire publication."

Their tagline is:

> A science fiction magazine where writers, designers and researchers of the past and present come together to explore the future.

Visions blends essays and short stories from both masters of the genre and newcomers to paint a provocative landscape of the future that anyone can enjoy and reflect on."

Their submission calls tend to be theme-based. The first issue was "Visions of Home" and the second issue "Visions of Humanity." The submission guidelines clarify:

"There are many definitions of science fiction but please note, we're not looking for paranormal, supernatural or fantasy stories.

> We're more inclined to favour pieces that emphasize the literary and reflective aspects of science fiction.

Strong language and imagery is allowed as long as it serves a clear purpose, however please do not send anything that has very graphic or gory scenes."

I sent a story in for the first call, and they send me a personalized rejection letter:

"We've reviewed Invasive Species and unfortunately it hasn't made the cut. It's a nice pitch that creates an interesting atmosphere, unfortunately the story doesn't fit with the rest of the commissioned pieces.

> Overall, the delivery didn't feel fully mastered and the narrative could have been snappier.

It left me wanting something a bit more crafted to create a more long-lasting impression. We're very thankful that you took the time to submit your story and hope you will consider us again."

Using this advice, I've rewritten Invasive Species (over and over again) and it has found a home with *DreamForge Anvil*.

Submit here:
https://www.readvisions.com/submission-guidelines

28

34 ORCHARD

ark Literary Fiction

Editor: Kristi Peterson Schoonover
　Pay: $50
　Word range: 1,000-7,500
　Simultaneous submissions? Yes
　Reprints? No
　Ezine - Based out of the US

~

Kristi Peterson Schoonover has been one of my most amazing finds in my exploration of speculative fiction. She has given me exceptional advice and has taken the time to communicate personally.

Her publication is a newer addition on the market and Schoonover says:

"There are two types of writing that I really love. Literary stories with prose that takes your breath away and transports you into another world.

> Then I also love to be scared, made uncomfortable and sometimes even shocked.

34 Orchard is a new literary on-line journal that combines both."

The website defines what they publish:

"At 34 Orchard, we like dark, intense pieces that speak to a deeper truth.

> We're not genre-specific; we just like scary, disturbing, unsettling, and sad.

We like things we can't put down and things that make us go "wow" when we've finished. But our main goal here at 34 Orchard is to publish the stuff we like to read, and you're not in our heads. So, don't over think it. Just submit. We are an international journal and welcome submissions from everyone, all over the world."

Though I haven't sold her any stories yet, she has taken the time to give me thoughtful advice. She even did some editing and plot suggestions for two of my pieces she rejected. I've submitted to *34 Orchard* four times.

"A Melody for Measure", "The Foreign Student", "The Black Hole of Enlightenment" and "Shafted" have all been turned down.

I asked her if I could resubmit "The Foreign Student" after I'd done some extensive editing on it and she replied:

"Actually, the reason we passed on this story didn't have anything to do with its quality (as is the case with most stories--many times, the reason the story doesn't get picked up for a publication has to do with that particular publication's vision). I enjoyed this story, but it's just not quite the "vibe" I'm looking for for 34 Orchard, and if you asked me exactly what that was, I couldn't tell you. I just know it when I see it. So, re-submitting it, in this case, won't make a difference.

> Most editors, when they love a story, will take it even if it has a few issues; these are things that can be worked on in the editing process.

I'm sure the improvements you made are fantastic! It should now have a better shot at a different publication.
I wish you the best of luck! You can feel free to submit a different story any time during our open call."

I self-published "A Melody for Measure" and "The Foreign Student". Schoonover took the time and gave me detailed edits for "Shafted" and "The Black Hole of Enlightenment." Her comments were so detailed; I am still working on the rewrites.

∽

Submit here:
https://34orchard.com/guidelines/

29

VASTERIEN

*L*iterary Horror Fiction

Editor: Matt Cardin
  Pay: 5 cents per word
  Word range: 750 - 6,000
  Simultaneous submissions? Not sure
  Reprints? No
  eBook and Print- Based out of the US

Vasterien magazine has a lush, gothic feel and is published by Grimscribe Press. They look for original work inspired by Ligottian themes. Thomas Ligotti is an American horror writer (born in 1953 and still living) known for weird fiction and philosophical horror, especially in the gothic tradition. His worldview is categorized as pessimistic and nihilistic.

> *The name Vasterien was drawn from Thomas Ligotti's classic story of the same title, which S. T. Joshi has characterized as "Ligotti's most searching exploration of the forbidden book theme.*

From the website:

"The word Vastarien means "the forbidden tome. The impossible otherworld. A textual entryway into a place where everything was transfixed in the order of the unreal. . .. Each passage he entered in the book both enchanted and appalled him with images and incidents so freakish and chaotic that his usual sense of these terms disintegrated along with everything else.

 Rampant oddity seemed to be the rule of the realm; imperfection became the source of the miraculous.

-wonders of deformity and marvels of miscreation. There was horror, undoubtedly. But it was a horror uncompromised by any feeling of lost joy or thwarted redemption; rather, it was a deliverance by damnation. And if Vastarien was a nightmare, it was a nightmare transformed in spirit by the utter absence of refuge: nightmare made normal."

The website lists their interests as:

- Supernatural horror (both fiction and film)
- Philosophical pessimism
- Gnosticism
- Buddhism
- Nihilism
- Surrealism
- Decadent and fin de siècle literature

- Pessimistic and morbid poetry (Trakl, Thomson, Brennan, Leopardi, Larkin, Wiloch, Barnitz, etc.)
- Aberrant psychology (depression, bipolar disorder, anxiety disorders, anhedonia...)
- Euthanasia/Right to Die
- Horror in the visual arts
- Antinatalism
- L'école belge de l'étrange
- Corporate degradation
- The architecture and topography of Detroit and its suburbs
- Horror and pessimism as it relates to most any field
- Any crossovers or hybrids of these categories/writers

They use submittable.com for submissions, and I received a declined through the system without any further notes for my story, "The Rougarou".

"The Rougarou" was rejected nine times and rewritten three times before being picked up by Soteira Press for the anthology series *The Monsters We Forgot*. You can read how that happened in *The Story Behind The Stories*.

I don't find *Vasterien* open very often for submissions.

Submit here:
https://grimscribepress.com/submission-guidelines/

30
APPARITION LIT

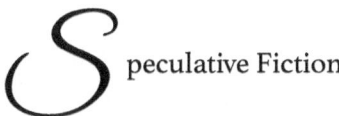peculative Fiction

Managing Editor: Tacoma Tomilson
   Pay: 3 cents per word
   Word range: 1,000-5,000
   Simultaneous submissions? No
   Reprints? No
   Ezine - International Staff

Apparition Lit asks for stories to conform to a theme for each issue.

   Previous themes for the last few calls were Experimentation; Transfiguration; Redemption; Satisfaction; Euphoria; Retribution; Ambition; and Resistance.

The website says:

"Speculative fiction is weird, almost unclassifiable. It's fantasy, sci-fi, horror, and literary.

> We want strange, misshapen stories with enough emotional heft to break a heart, with prose that's as clear and delicious as broth.

We love proactive characters and settings that feel lived in and real enough to touch. Stories with style, stories with emotion, stories with character. We want it all."

I've had four rejections from this market, and here is my most positive one. Their response time is very good.

"Thank you for submitting "THE CORP" to Apparition Literary Magazine. Your work made it to the second round of consideration. Our editors closely reviewed your story, but ultimately decided not to accept it for publication. We wish you the best of luck submitting it elsewhere and would love to see more of your work in the future."

"The Corp" has yet to find a home, and is being extended to novella length.

Submit here:
https://apparitionlit.com/submissions/

31

TRANSLUNAR TRAVELLERS LOUNGE

un Speculative Fiction

Editor: Aimee Ogden
 Editor: Bennett North
 Pay: 3 cents per word
 Word range: up to 5,000
 Simultaneous submissions? No
 Ezine and eBook- Based out of US

Who doesn't want to submit to a venue that's looking for fun? Just the name alone of this magazine is absolutely brilliant. *Translunar Travelers Lounge* is published twice a year and asks for stories that explore the fun side of fantasy and science fiction.

From the website:

"Put down your bags, take a seat, and relax with our fine selection of short fiction. Broadly defined, the type of fiction we are looking for is "fun". Yes, that descriptor is highly subjective, and ultimately it comes down to the personal preferences of the editors. However, here are a few road signs to get you started on the path into our hearts.

> A fun story, at its core, is one that works on the premise that things aren't all bad; that ultimately, good wins out.

This doesn't necessarily mean that your story has to be silly or lighthearted (though it certainly can be). Joy can be made all the more powerful when juxtaposed against tragedy. In the end, though, there should be hope, and we want stories that are truly fun for as many different kinds of people as possible.

> Swashbuckling adventure, deadly intrigue, and gleeful romance are some of the most obvious examples of what we're looking for,

but we won't say no to more subtle or complicated topics, as long as they fit under the wider "fun" umbrella."

They are open annually for submissions from March 15th through April 15th for the August issue, and from September 15th through October 15th for the February issue.

I've sent three stories to them, and they've sent me a standard rejection, usually in less than a month.

"Thank you for sharing "The Foreign Student" with us. While we enjoyed reading it, it's unfortunately not what we're looking for right now. We appreciate your interest in our magazine and hope you'll try us again next time."

"The Foreign Student" was rejected 22 times before I self-published it as "The Lore of Lust".

Submit here:
https://translunartravelerslounge.com/submissions/

32

THREE-LOBED BURNING EYE

*H*orror, Wonder, and the Weird

Editor: Andrew S. Fuller
　Pay: $100 for short fiction, $30 for flash
　Word range: 1,001-7,500
　Simultaneous submissions? No
　Reprints? No
　Ezine and Print - Based out of the US

Three-Lobed Burning Eye is a speculative fiction magazine offered free on-line. They publish twice a year, with a print anthology every other year. Each issue features six short stories.

　The guidelines describe what they are looking for:

"Original speculative fiction: horror, fantasy, science fiction. We're looking for short stories from across the big classifications and those shadowy places between: magical realism, fantastique, slipstream, interstitial, and the weird tale. We will consider suspense or western, though we prefer it contain some speculative element.

> We like voices that are full of feeling, from literary to pulpy, with styles unique and flowing, but not too experimental.

All labels aside, we want tales that expand genre, that value imagination in character, narrative, and plot. We want to see something new and different."

Each issue also includes audio readings, and authors can record their own stories. The editor advises avoiding extreme horror or pure erotica. Writers must be 18 years old or older. More advice includes:

"Read widely in the science fiction, fantasy, horror, mystery, and other genres.

> Beware clichés, overused language, hackneyed plots, cheap thrills, thin characters, and wish fulfillment.

There is nothing wrong with tropes and trends like vampires, werewolves, ghosts, zombies, serial killers, faeries, superheroes, or aliens; but we are interested in new explorations of ideas. Don't rely on cleverness and twists. Strive for depth, texture, and imagination."

I sent them my story "Death Metal Fan" about an evil room fan that slowly corrupts a young woman.
Here was a rejection I received from this magazine:

"Thank you for sending your story to Three-lobed Burning Eye magazine. Unfortunately, we have decided not to accept it for publication. We regret that we cannot offer more feedback and wish you the best in finding a home for this piece."

"Death Metal Fan" was one of my first sales. You can read about its journey in *The Story Behind The Stories*.

∼

Submit here:
https://www.3lobedmag.com/submitform.html

33
LAMPLIGHT

ark Fiction

Editor: Jacob Haddon
  Pay: 3 cents per word
  Word range: up to 7,000
  Simultaneous submissions? Yes
  Reprints? Yes, 1 cent per word
  eBook and Print - Based out of the US

Lamplight Magazine asks writers to look to *The Twilight Zone* and *The Outer Limits* for inspiration.

"We are a literary magazine of dark fiction, both short stories and flash fiction. We want your best. But then, doesn't everyone? No specific sub-genres or themes, just good stories. For inspiration, we suggest "The Twilight Zone", "The Outer Limits", and Lamplight, Vol1 Issue 1 which is free.

> We go for stories that are dark, literary; we are looking for the creepy, the weird and the unsettling.

We do not accept stories with the following: vampires, zombies, werewolves, serial killers, hitmen, excessive gore or sex, excessive abuse against women, revenge fantasies, cannibals, high fantasy."

I've submitted three stories to this market and it took just over three months to receive my rejection for "Death Metal Fan". This is the note I received through submittable.com

"Thank you for your submission to Lamplight Magazine. We regret that we are unable to publish 'Death Metal Fan' We are grateful for the opportunity to consider it, and we wish you the best of luck in placing it elsewhere."

"Death Metal Fan" was picked up after being rejected 7 times by other markets by *hauntedmtl.com*. The other two stories I submitted to this market, "The Last Ride" and "The New Mutants" were picked up before I heard back from *Lamplight*, so I withdrew them.
"The Last Ride" was published in *The Corona Book of Ghost Stories,* and "The New Mutants" is in Third Flatiron's *Gotta Wear Eclipse Glasses*.
There are two submission periods for *Lamplight*.
March 15– May 15 for the September and December Issues
September 15– November 15 for March and June Issues

Submit here:
https://lamplightmagazine.submittable.com/submit

34

NEO-OPSIS SCIENCE FICTION MAGAZINE

Fantasy & Science Fiction

Editor: Karl Johanson
    Editor: Stephanie Johanson
    Pay: 2.5 cents per word
    Word range: prefers under 6,000
    Simultaneous submissions? No
    Ezine and Print - Based out of Canada

Neo-opsis is a digital Canadian magazine run out of Victoria, British Columbia and has been publishing since 2003. The first 30 issues are available in print. Along with short fiction, you'll find science and nature articles, plus book and movie reviews.

From the website:

 What is Neo-opsis Science Fiction Magazine about?

Entertainment – Let Neo-opsis magazine entertain you with fun and interesting stories, written from the perspective of science and fantasy.
Information – Read informative articles on science and nature. Check out the Science and Science Fiction news articles.
Interpretation – Enjoy book and movie reviews. Find out what others think, with Neo-opsis opinion columns and letters section.

They give a fairly standard rejection letter, but I found it interesting I was the 7111th submission.

"Thank you for giving us the chance to consider your story. "Invasive Species" is the 7111th submission received by Neo-opsis Science Fiction Magazine since its start in 2003. "Invasive Species" does not fit our needs, but thank you again for your submission."

"Invasive Species" is with *DreamForge Anvil*, and has more hours into revising it then all my other stories put together.

Submit here:
http://www.neo-opsis.ca/guidelines.htm

35

INTERZONE

New Science Fiction & Fantasy

Editor: Andy Cox
   Pay: rumored a British penny per word
   Word range: up to 10,000
   Simultaneous submissions? No
   Reprints? No
   Print - Based out of the UK

Interzone is a highly respected market for Speculative Fiction writers, and is the eighth longest-running English language Sci-Fi magazine in history.

> *Interzone is renowned for publishing award-winning fiction and has been credited with creating a resurgence of interest in science fiction within the UK.*

Interzone is one of three magazines published by TTA Press. The website explains:

"The publisher is named after the magazine it founded in 1994, The Third Alternative, which was renowned for its slipstream/horror fiction. The Third Alternative is now known as Black Static. We also publish Interzone, Britain's longest running science fiction and fantasy magazine, plus a series of novellas showcasing longer works by some of TTA's best known and most admired contributors and the anthology series Crimewave."

All three of my stories have received standard rejections:

"Many thanks for sending 'The New Mutants", but I'm afraid it's not quite right for Interzone. Sorry to disappoint this time but please send us another story soon."

"The New Mutants" was picked up by Third Flatiron for their anthology about bright futures, *Gotta Wear Eclipse Glasses*.
Listen to The New Mutants

Submit here:
TTA Press uses Submittable.com for all submissions.
https://tta.submittable.com/submit

36

SEXY FANTASTIC MAGAZINE

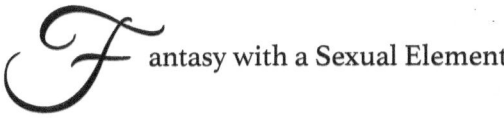antasy with a Sexual Element

Editor: Robert Zoltan
  Pay: $100
  Word range: 3,000-15,000
  Simultaneous submissions? Yes
  Reprints? Yes, 2 cents per word
  Ezine and Print - Based out of US

Sexy Fantastic Magazine is a new addition to the market and has an interesting slant to it.

From the website:

"Sexy Fantastic is an Art, Literature and Culture magazine for adults, specializing in the genres of Science Fiction and Fantasy. Each month the magazine presents fiction stories, non-fiction articles like book and movie discussions, artwork, photography and other features.

> This is a sex positive magazine, and emphasis is given to work of an erotic, sexual, or romantic nature,

although not all the content will be of that kind, for the greatest emphasis is on quality, regardless of sexual content. Contributors who wish to create work that is not censored by the mainstream publishing industry will find Sexy Fantastic to be a new market for them.

> Readers who are looking for tasteful, superb, uncensored mainstream entertainment for mature adults will enjoy this magazine.

You will find that Sexy Fantastic is a less violent magazine than most mainstream science fiction and fantasy books and magazines.

> We frown on gratuitous violence or gore and it will not find its way into this magazine.

Sexy Fantastic also is not interested in nihilistic or despairing works, but seeks to publish creative works that amuse, inspire, move, spark imagination, challenge, provoke thought, and entertain.
Our main mission is to create and publish the absolutely highest quality of creative work possible every month. Our goals are to bring a little bit of joy, meaning and happiness into people's lives, and to help bring healthy eroticism into the mainstream."

They do things a little differently and ask for writers to submit the first 500 words of their story, and if the readers are intrigued, then you can send in your whole story. They ask for writers to send in fiction loosely based on themes.

> Issue #1, "Secret Agents, Time Travelers & Other Dimensions."
> The theme for Issue #2 is "Goddesses, Nymphs and Supervixens."

I sent in one of my more recent creations, "The Museum of the Lost People", and Robert Zoltan did ask to be sent the rest of the story:

> "Thanks for the submission. Can you please send me the full story?"

However, he didn't choose it for his publication. A note here, Zoltan does not send out rejection letters. When I queried, he was very pleasant and chatted with me about how he created his amazing website. (Check it out, Zoltan is a professional illustrator and designer.) However, he said:

> "I usually only respond if I accept a story, because I'm handling so much with the magazine that I need to only do the work that's absolutely necessary. And since I accept simultaneous submissions, you can always send elsewhere at the same time."

Submit here:
https://sexyfantasticmagazine.com/fictionsubmissions/

37

PARABNORMAL

aranormal Fiction

Editor: H. David Blalock
   Pay: $25
   Word range: 3000-6000
   Simultaneous submissions? No
   Reprints? Yes, $7 per story
   Print - Based out of US

ParABnormal is a publication created by Hiraeth Books and is open to short stories, poetry, art, articles, and reviews on a set submission schedule:

Submissions are accepted Febraury 1 – March 31, June 1 – July 31, October 1 – November 30.

From the website:

"The subject matter of parABnormal Magazine is, yes, the paranormal. For us, this includes ghosts, spectres, haunts, various whisperers, and so forth. It also includes shapeshifters and creatures from various folklores.

> Creatures like vampires, werewolves, and zombies are not paranormal.

Shapeshifters, for the purpose of this magazine, refer to the spiritual shift, not the physical. Think Native American shaman. Paranormal activity centers around the human, not the creature.
Please, no stories that involve excessive blood, gore, digestive tracts, and so forth. If you write a dark story, make sure it is spooky.

> Makes sure it is a story that should be read with all the lights on, with the reader looking over his or her shoulder while turning the pages.

However, we are not interested in zombie stories for this publication.
We continue to get submissions about vampires, werewolves, zombies, and ghouls. These are supernatural creatures, not paranormal. Please do not send them. Psychic vampires, undead, anything similar to a generic supernatural creature is a very hard sell and will most likely be rejected. Just saving you and us the time and aggravation."

I've sent them two stories, "Quiver" and "The Foreign Student" and received standard rejection letters from them in about a month:

"Thank you for allowing us to review your story, but we don't think it would be a good fit for us. We look forward to hearing from you in future."

Neither of these stories has found homes yet.

Submit here:
https://www.hiraethsffh.com/parabnormal-magazine-guidelines

38

PULP MODERN

ulp Fiction

Editor: Alec Cizak
　Pay: $25
　Word range: 3,500 - 5,000
　Simultaneous submissions? No
　Reprints? No
　Print - Based out of the US

Pulp Modern publishes crime, fantasy, science fiction, horror and westerns and believes in "true and absolute freedom of speech."

　"NO SUBJECT is taboo," the submission guidelines state.

　Alec Cizak is the man behind the magazine and he says "I started publishing Pulp Modern because I didn't see any journals at the time that brought the major genres together. I also didn't see any big-time publications publishing riskier stories, so I felt there was a need for a market that could take chances since no advertising dollars were on the line."

Cizak also says his magazine is full of:

 "gut-honest stories about junkies, pimps, and hookers."

Though it is a financially losing venture, he keeps his magazine going because:

"There are many, many writers out there. Some of them are really good and they don't have connections in the publishing world. A journal like Pulp Modern is there to make sure those unheard voices are heard."

Pulp Modern is also starting up *Pulp Modern Flash*:

"Pulp Modern will be launching a new flash fiction site for all pulp genres (crime/noir, horror, science fiction, fantasy, adventure, and western) called Pulp Modern Flash. Stories should be 1000 words or less.
There are no rules here as far as subject matter.

 We ENCOURAGE hardcore fiction.

We are NOT interested in being lectured and talked down to; mainstream publishing is all about that and there are plenty of places to send that kind of work. We want to read STORIES that ALL human beings can relate to.
We are unable to pay at this time. However, stories we deem above and beyond excellent will be invited to be included in an eventual anthology (for which authors will be paid)."

I've had one story picked up by Cizak. You can find "A Time to Forget" in the *Pulp Modern: Tech Noir special* and read about its journey in *The Story Behind The Stories.*

Submit here:
http://pulp-modern.blogspot.com

39

ECONOCLASH REVIEW

ulp Fiction

∿

Editor: J.D. Graves
Pay: $25
Word range: max 1,500 to 4,500
Simultaneous submissions? Yes
Reprints? No
Print - based out of the US

∿

Econoclash Review promises Quality Cheap Thrills. If you are looking for stories about:

> "shady casino hosts, murderous junkies, pregnant prom queens, strange kaiju cults, small town larceny and Sasquatch love brides."

From the website:

"EconoClash Review believes in free speech and wants to provide our readers with a much needed escape into other worlds.

> We like stories about Weirdos, Criminals and Pregnant Prom Queens going to great lengths to destroy or keep the status quo.

HOWEVER, we don't want erotica, or pornography, or torture-porn-erotica between characters of any age, race, species both real or fictional. Nothing gratuitous. Avoid the tropes best you can. Just because we want GENRE doesn't mean we want STALE."

I sent them a story about a Rasta Fairy called "High Adventure":

"Thank you for allowing me to read your work. I really enjoyed the quality of the writing and the fairy tale aspect of the story. However, I felt like the third act was missing that certain punch. I kept expecting the turn.

> It seemed to be building to some event which it did not occur. The stakes for me were just not high enough.

Just one reader's opinion. While I appreciate your work, I don't think it's right for ECR in its present state. I wouldn't mind reading a revised version of this story or something else from you during a future open sub call. Best of luck with your work."

I rewrote the story, adding in a bloody climax with creatures of the fantasy world, and J.D. Graves accepted it.

Submit here:

https://www.econoclash.com/p/econoclash-quality-cheap-thrills-is.html

40

ELECTRIC SPEC

Science Fiction, Fantasy & the Macabre

Editor: Nikki Baird
 Pay: $20
 Word range: 250 - 7,000
 Simultaneous submissions? No
 Reprints? Yes, 2 cents per word
 Ezine - Based out of US

Electric Spec has been around for over 11 years, don't use slush readers, and pride themselves on giving every story they publish a good edit. They define themselves as:

> "Electric Spec is a not-for-profit speculative fiction magazine published four times per year. Our primary goal is getting

great speculative fiction into the hands (or screens) of readers. Since 2005, we've been publishing short stories from authors all over the world. We've worked with all kinds of authors, from published professionals to new writers. We also believe in the value of the editorial process, and we edit every story we publish."

I've sent six stories to this publication and one was held for consideration but ultimately rejected. My responses took around four weeks. This is the first email I received about a story called "The Writing Retreat":

Thank you for submitting your story to Electric Spec. The editors have reviewed it and decided to hold it for voting. We anticipate making our final selection of stories for our May issue in early May. We will notify you as soon as a final decision has been made."

Then this:

"Thank you for submitting your story to Electric Spec. Unfortunately, your story does not meet our needs at this time. Yours is one of many high-quality submissions we received, and we encourage you to try us again if you have another story that you think would be a good fit."

"The Writing Retreat" was eventually picked up by an anthology called *Strangely Funny VII* by Mystery and Horror, LLC. You can read about that story's journey in *The Publishers Behind the Pages*.

They have reading periods for each issue, and never close to submissions.

- February closes January 15
- May closes April 15

- August closes July 15
- November closes October 15

Submit here:
https://www.electricspec.com/Submissions.html

41

ALLEGORY

cience Fiction, Fantasy & Horror

Managing Editor: Ty Drago
   Pay: $15
   Word range: 500 - 5,000
   Simultaneous submissions? Yes
   Reprints? No
   Ezine - Based out of the US

Allegory is a biannual online magazine, and they feature some outstanding authors. I've found the staff approachable and Senior Editor Jessica Bayliss has gone above and beyond in helping me understand their market.

From the website:

We're looking for good, solid fiction. We specialize in the Science Fiction, Fantasy and Horror genres.

We will consider other genres, such as humor or general interest, provided that the work possesses an original, "quirky" slant.

Here are some basic do's and don'ts.

- DO give us strong characters and good plotting. DO put clever, but logical twists on the end of your tales. DO experiment with new ideas and unusual writing styles, but without falling into traps of contrivance and cliché.
- DON'T submit any stories based on movies, television or any printed media not your own. DON'T submit reprints without including the name of the publication in which the work first appeared, along with the date of publication.
- DON'T send more than one story in the same submission."

These are the rejections I have received from them for a story called "Three Calendars".

"Thank you for sharing your story with us. This was a really beautiful story.

 I love the way you tell this mystery within the context of your character's dementia.

I don't know if it has quite enough of a speculative element, but I'm going to forward it on for further review by our editor. Congrats on making it to the next stage!"

Then I received this one...

"I hate writing this letter. I deeply regret to inform you that "Three Calendars" did not make the final cut for Volume 35/62 of ALLEGORY. Please understand that we received nearly 600 submissions for this issue and narrowed that down to only 54 finalists. ALL of those finalists are strong, quality stories - any of which we would be pleased and honored to publish.

> The final list of twelve is made by comparing the stories, more with an eye toward issue balance than the merits of one story over another.

Your tale is a GREAT piece, and I'm very very sorry that we can't use it. For whatever it may be worth, we would like to include your name and the title of your story in the Honorable Mentions section of our main page. Feel free to use this as a recommendation of your work to other markets. Again, my apologies. And good luck with your writing efforts."

"Three Calendars" was picked up by *Ellery Queen Mystery Magazine*, becoming my first pro sale. You can read more about this tale and its journey in *The Story Behind The Stories*.

I then sent *Allegory* three more of my stories, and they were all rejected. But Bayliss writes a fantastic letter:

"Thank you for sharing your story with us (and it's lovely to see another story of yours).

> This piece was really fun. I have a particular fondness for fancy poultry, and I love your voice here.

I didn't think it was quite right for Allegory, though. It felt ... incomplete? It's hard to put this one into words. The way the birds took up instruments w/o much of a process--so easily and simply--made it feel too, for lack of a better word, easy. It might work better if the chickens have some time to brood over the potential for a terrible future fate and then, along the way, catch on to the notion of their musical potential. That would actually build up tension and it would make the formation of the band feel more believable (to whatever extent 4 chickens playing music can ever be believable, but you get my point)."

I couldn't find anyone to buy "Farmyard Follies", so I self-published it. Please read *Allegory's* guidelines carefully before sending them a story.

∼

Submit here:
   https://www.allegoryezine.com/submissions

42

SWITCHBLADE

Hardboiled Noir

Editor: Scotch Rutherford
  Pay: $15 US
  Word range: max 4,500
  Simultaneous submissions? No
  Reprints? No
  Print- Based out of the US

Switchblade calls itself outlaw fiction, and produces anthologies. Modern Noir, rural noir, urban noir... they want stories where your criminal is your protagonist.

If you like to write about hookers, enforcers, drug dealers, porn stars, junkies and pimps, this is your market.

From the website:

"Think Richard Stark, Ross MacDonald, Jim Thompson, Don Winslow, Ken Bruen, James Ellroy, Lawrence Block, Iceberg Slim, Max Allan Collins, Christa Faust. (just to name a few) We don't do cozies. We don't do procedurals. We're not a literary magazine, and we don't do other genres. That said, we will consider noir/crime fiction ranging from the early twentieth century up to present day. Aside from that, we are a no limit hardboiled fiction journal—

 we publish the kind of stories no one else will consider.

Back in the day there was a Nynex yellow pages ad campaign that went like this: if it's out there, it's in here—that's how we feel.

 The world is filled with deviance, and good hardboiled fiction reflects that.

We like strong characters, and good story telling, and we will not reject anyone based on mainstream morality. Amoral protagonists are encouraged. We will not however, publish masturbation fodder for masochistic pedophiles. We're not interested in torture-porn erotica. But if you've got a deplorable protagonist, and there's a good story—we'll print it."

I responded to one of their anthology calls and ended up having a story called "A Time to Forget" in the *Pulp Modern: Tech Noir* special, a joint project between *Pulp Modern* and *Switchblade*. To learn more about the journey of that story, pick up *The Story Behind The Stories*.

Submit here:
http://www.switchblademag.com

43

NOVEL NOCTULE

*L*iterary Horror

Editor-in-chief: Jacqueline Dyre
Pay: $10 US
Word range: up to 10,000
Simultaneous submissions? No
Reprints? Query first
Ezine - Based out of US

Novel Noctule is an online, monthly magazine and a fairly new venue for authors and artists to submit work. Their tagline?

The Night Welcomes You.

I've found them responsive and approachable.

The website says:

 We use horror to shed light on the human condition.

Issues contain two or three original stories, poetry, artwork, creator spotlights, and related works of terror. Our stories are often categorized in the new weird genre. We publish on the 28th of each month. Our most recent issue launched on November 28th, 2020: We are currently accepting submissions on a rolling basis!"

Before *Novel Noctule*, I'd never heard the term "new weird horror". It refers to a movement in the literary world that came about in the 1990s through early 2000s from horror authors who cross genre boundaries. Stories often combine fantasy elements, existential and physical terror, and science fiction.

They are looking for:

 Horror with a message, with a strong preference for new weird horror.

Any variant. This, meaning that we will accept anything from supernatural, goblin-ghoul-zombie-thumping-in-the-night types of works to more subtle, mundane terrors."

Here is one of three rejection letters I received from Jacqueline Dyre:

"Although we decided not to include this piece in our publication, we felt that the concept behind "A Deadful Friday the 13th" was engaging! That being said, the execution could have been better. Some sentences were a bit awkward and your descriptors could have been chosen with more care.

More attention might also be given to the believability of the dialogue

(for instance, a gang member probably wouldn't say, "I'm gonna get my gang members after that biotch"). We hope that you'll submit again!"

I laughed when I read this rejection letter. Dyre was right. My dialogue needed a serious overhaul. I still haven't found a home for "A Deadful Friday the 13th", but I did improve my "gang speech".

Submit here:
https://www.novelnoctule.com/submissions

44

THE HOUSE OF ZOLO JOURNAL OF SPECULATIVE LITERATURE

 peculative Literature

Editors: Erika Steeves & Nihls Anderson
    Pay: 10 cents per word
    Word range: not listed
    Simultaneous submissions? No
    Reprints? Yes
    eBook and Print - based out of Canada

The House of Zolo is a newer market founded in 2019 by an independent Canadian publisher.
    From the website:

> "HOZ is looking for literature that explores possibilities for the future.

We want challenging short stories that are character driven, that reimagine the world and our place in it.

We are looking for radical authors, feminist authors, LGBTQ2S authors, authors who experiment. Themes that thrill us: transhumanism, artificial intelligence, genetic engineering, new systems, resistance, activism, queer perspectives, feminist perspectives, nature.
We are not interested in stories that concern the reinvention of empire, rehashing of old narratives, or excessive violence. We entertain all genre-based stories so long as they concern the future and especially if related to our favourite themes."

I've had two rejections from this market. I sent them my story "Camp Blue Marble", and got this back three months later:

"We received so many excellent submissions to our call and we were forced to make some tough choices. We're sorry that we could not place your story during this round. We recognize that you are a talented writer and want you to know that the entire Editorial Team read your piece and were impressed by your writing. It just wasn't a fit this time."

"Camp Blue Marble" was published as "Camp Napanoo" in an anthology called *Unreal*.

Submit here:
https://houseofzolo.com/submit-to-hoz/

45

DARK MATTER MAGAZINE

 cience Fiction

Editor-in-chief: Rob Carroll
 Pay: 8 cents per word
 Word range: 1,000-5,000
 Simultaneous submissions? Yes
 Reprints? Yes, 2 cents per word
 Ezine and Print - Based out of US

This is a new player in the science fiction market, and they plan on publishing six issues per year.
 From the website:

"Dark Matter Magazine was started during the COVID-19 lock-down of 2020. It is the brainchild of a dedicated group of science fiction enthusiasts with professional backgrounds in trade publishing, peer-reviewed science journals, marketing, corporate communications, broadcast news media, television, information technology, computer science, and graphic design. We hope to grow Dark Matter into one of the premier science fiction storytelling outlets on the market today."

They ask for:

 Stories that explore the shadow side of reality.

This does not mean that we prefer gratuitous sex and violence, or that the story must be cynical or misanthropic. Even stories of hope and optimism can arrive at their theses after first taking us on a journey through the most downtrodden fringes of society, or the deepest reaches of space, or the darkest corners of the mind. But stories don't always have happy endings either."

I sent a story in for the first issue and received a rejection:

"Thank you for allowing us to read "Invasive Species." Unfortunately, the story doesn't fit our needs at the moment. We wish you success in finding the right outlet for your work"

"Invasive Species" is in the hands of *DreamForge Anvil*.

Submit here:
https://darkmattermagazine.com/submission-guidelines/

46

BONE YARD SOUP MAGAZINE

*H*orror & Dark Fantasy

Editor: T.L. Spezia
Pay: 5 cents per word
Word range: 2,000-6,000
Simultaneous submissions? Yes
Reprints? Yes, 1 cent per word
Ezine - Based out of US

Boneyard Soup Magazine is a new player in the digital space. They launched January 2021, and promise to be weird, morbid, and macabre.

From the website:

"Boneyard Soup Magazine is a horror and dark fantasy publication. Our mission is twofold: to publish the finest short stories from across the entire genre and to support new and emerging writers in order to bring fresh perspectives to horror literature.

> Horror engages humanity's darkest fears, anxieties, worries; it peeks behind the curtain and treads where few other genres will.

Horror speaks volumes about the human condition, while scaring the bejesus out of us. We hope to live up to this mission with each and every issue of our magazine. Published quarterly in a digital format, Boneyard Soup Magazine seeks to feature stories and original artwork which reflect the many subgenres of Horror--from dark fantasy, to traditional monsters, gothic, the weird, and more. We hope to be the authors of your newest nightmares. Sweet dreams."

The submission guidelines add:

We publish in the horror and dark fantasy genres and are open to almost anything you can imagine within those categories.

> Traditional Gothic. Pulpy horror with an '80s vibe. Body horror. Ghost stories. Horror comedy.

Don't be afraid to submit if your tale falls within the horror and dark fantasy genres. However, we are not interested in stories with extreme violence or overt sexual themes."

I sent "The Patron Saint of Livestock" in for their first issue in October, 2020. In less than two months, this was the rejection I received:

"Thank you again for your interest in Boneyard Soup Magazine and for allowing us to review your story submission. Unfortunately, the story does not meet our editorial needs at this time. We receive story submissions on a daily basis and the limited space in our magazine means we must reject the majority of what we receive. This makes editorial decisions all the more difficult and frustrating. We sincerely hope your story finds a home soon, and that you'll consider submitting more work in the future."

"The Patron Saint of Livestock" found a home as an eldritch story with *Cosmic Roots & Eldritch Shores*.

Submit here:
https://www.boneyardsoup.com/submit

47

THE CURIOUSER

Magic Realism

~

Editor: Thomas Bailey
    Pay: $50-$140 per story (Australian)
    Word range: 600-6,000
    Simultaneous submissions? Yes
    Reprints? No
    Ezine- Based out of Australia

~

Curiouser Magazine has a great tagline:

> "*Strange Words for Strange Times.*"

This is another digital magazine born out of 2020. The website says:

> We love the fantastical, the horrific, the experimental, the incantatory.

We don't like morality plays, overt spiritualism, the banal, the painfully self-aware.
As stated, we're looking for stories that excite, that break the boundary between real and unreal. Experimentation and surreal ways of looking at the world we live in will be looked upon fondly.

> Horror, magic realism, speculative fiction and streams of consciousness are welcome – but they must be somewhat grounded in real life.

We have no issue with sex, violence or profanity – this is, after all, a journal made by and for adults – but as with most things, excess isn't quite becoming."

I've sent them two stories, both about my leech man Seth with "The Attack of the Leech People" and "The Metamorphosis" but unfortunately, this magazine does not send rejections. So, if you don't hear from them in four weeks after the submission window closes, you can assume you were unsuccessful.

"The Metamorphosis" was picked up by *Scare Street*, and "The Attack of the Leech People" is being reworked.

Submit here:
https://curiousermag.com/submissions/

48

THE COMMON TONGUE

ark Fantasy

Editor-in-chief: Kade Draven Freeland
   Pay: 3 cents per word
   Word range: 600-6,000
   Simultaneous submissions? Yes
   Reprints? No
   Ezine- Based out of the US

The first issue of *The Common Tongue* releases March 2021. The darkness of 2020 has definitely inspired a spat of fun new places for writers to submit their work. From the website:

> "The Common Tongue Magazine (commontonguezine.com) is a dark fantasy & dark speculative fiction online magazine that publishes anthologies of masterfully told

fantasy short stories set in fascinating and extremely perilous fantasy worlds.

We publish roughly 60,000 words per issue five times a year. We publish work from authors of many backgrounds and cultures, promote underrepresented authors in fiction, publish work of writers whose voices give better understanding of cultures, human interconnectivity, and social issues in the world, while offering services based on merit and literacy excellence.

 Our tales are a different perspective on dark fantasy worlds as told by different voices.

Each writer has their own interpretation of their fantasy world, and it is their inspirations and their passion for storytelling that illuminates these worlds and the countless others that our imaginative minds create."

 "The magazine is a more than just a magazine – it's a biography of fantastic alternate universes that loom just a shade darker than ours.

It is meant to be a hub for speculative fiction in dark, dangerous fantasy worlds that force one to think outside of divine or magical intervention."

We do not consider our worlds anything less than or more than any other fictional worlds, but we are extremely proud that these worlds are unlike any others because we, as a community of writers and artists, have collaborated together to forge them. Each writer endows their own culture, experiences, and background into their tales, and we represent many different talents and cultures in our chosen tales."

I submitted a story to *The Common Tongue*, but then had to withdraw "The Metamorphosis" when it was picked up by *Scare Street*.

Submit here:
https://www.commontonguezine.com/submissions/

49

PLANET SCUMM

izarre Science Fiction

Editor: Sean Clancy
   Pay: 2 cents per word
   Word range: 2,000-6,000
   Simultaneous submissions? Yes
   Reprints? No
   Print - Based out of the US

How do you beat the name *Planet Scumm*? Plus, they have a retro 80's look to their website. This science fiction magazine is published by Spark & Fizz Books. As this guide goes to print, they have 11 issues and their Facebook page was created in February, 2017.

From the website:

"On Planet Scumm, we want to read stories that are different

and unexpected. Stories that introduce new ideas, or that look at old ideas with a fresh perspective.
They are looking for:

> Hard sci-fi, soft sci-fi, sci-fi that melts in your mouth-brain not your hand-brain.
>
> Speculative fiction, weird fiction, slipstream Basically anything that pleases Scummy, our megaphone-toting slime buddy, will be considered for entry to the interstellar archive aboard Scummy's saucer."

I submitted "A Deadful Friday the 13th" to them on October 30, 2020, and am still waiting for an answer.

Submit here:
https://www.planetscumm.space/submit

50

THE WEIRD AND WHATNOT

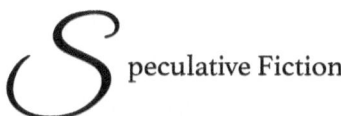peculative Fiction

Editors: Valerie, Joshua, and Farlee
   Pay: $10
   Word range: max 10,000
   Simultaneous submissions? Yes
   Reprints? No
   Ezine and Podcast- based out of the US

The Weird and Whatnot invites readers to explore the weirder side of things. They are looking for science fiction, fantasy, alternative history, magical realism, slipstream and paranormal horror.
   The website says:

"Valerie, Joshua, and Faralee met in a Utah Valley University advanced editing class. All three discovered an addiction to editing as part of that experience, and it was this shared adoration (along with a love for Hitchhiker's Guide to the Galaxy) which brought the three together in this SF Magazine & Community. They each contribute their own unique personality, experience, and skills, making a diverse and expert editing team."

I sent them my dystopian story about a future ruled by social media:

"Thank you for your interest in being published at The Weird and Whatnot. We have completed our review of "Live Free or Die," and we saw great potential in your work. Unfortunately, we found that it is not in line with the vision of our magazine and we cannot accept it for publication. Please don't take this as a blanket rejection. We would love to hear more from you in the future."

"Live Free or Die" was published by The World Writers Collective when it came 3rd in a contest.

Submit here:
http://www.theweirdandwhatnot.com

51

FROST ZONE ZINE

*H*orror, Speculative, & Literary

Editor: M.M. Macleod
　Pay: $5 or one contributor copy
　Word range: 600-3,000
　Simultaneous submissions? Yes
　Reprints? No
　Ezine and Print - based out of Canada

Frost Zone Zine is a quarterly anthology and wants spooky stories and eerie poetry. Their first issue was published in September, 2020.

　The website says:

> "The range of story types sought is broad: classic, gothic, supernatural, quiet, and psychological horror, near-future dystopian tales, other speculative fiction, realistic terror

(extreme weather, danger in nature, being lost – to name a few), dark folklore and fairytale, dark fantasy, dark literary fiction, and more."

They use greensubmissions.com and my rejection was posted there:

Thank you for submitting "The Black Hole of Enlightenment". We will not be moving forward with this story, but wish you the best of luck with your writing."

"The Black Hole of Enlightenment" has been rejected approximately 14 times and is still looking for a home.

Submit here:
https://frostzonezine.com/submissions/

52

NEW MYTHS

Magic Realism

Editor: Susan Shell Winston
   Pay: 1.5c per word
   Word range: 600-6000
   Simultaneous submissions? Yes
   Reprints? No
   Ezine- Based out of US

NewMyths is a quarterly ezine and has been publishing since 2007.

Their submission period is from January 1 through February 28 and from June 1 through July 31 of every year.

They publish all types of speculative fiction except graphic horror.

From the website:

"We like to balance each quarterly issue between science fiction and fantasy, dark and light, serious and humorous, hard and soft science, and longer and shorter works. Our readers are not fixated on a single style or tone or genre, but prefer a quality sample of the field.

> Think a combo plate of appetizers rather than a whole lot of popcorn."

I've sent them five stories and received standard rejections in good time:

"Thank you so much for thinking of NewMyths. Unfortunately, "A Deadful Friday the 13th" is not quite what we're looking for at this time. We wish you the best of luck placing it elsewhere."

"A Deadful Friday the 13th" is still looking for a home; it's my second zombie story.

∼

Submit here:
https://sites.google.com/a/newmyths.com/nmwebsite/submissions/sub-2

PART II
FLASH FICTION MARKETS

53

DAILY SCIENCE FICTION

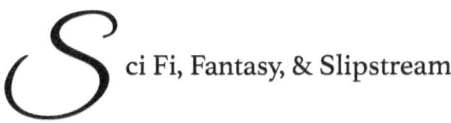Sci Fi, Fantasy, & Slipstream

Editor: Jonathan Laden
    Pay: 8 cents per word
    Word range: 100 - 1,500
    Simultaneous submissions? No
    Reprints? No
    Ezine - Based out of US

Daily Science Fiction is a big player in the short fiction market for speculative writers. It has been publishing science fiction through email and on-line since 2010. The name doesn't lie, it publishes stories every weekday.

    Hints from the editor:

We need short short fiction, especially flash fiction. Among our featured stories, a shorter tale will get an extra nudge on the scale when weighed against a longer one. This is both for financial reasons and because it matches the preferences of a plurality of our readership. Not fair? Perhaps. Consider yourself forewarned.

 Of course, we want your stories to ooze originality, but a well-written story is a must.

We are fond of character-driven fiction, though readers point out that not every story we publish fits that rubric. Our goal is to publish the best stories we can that will be interesting, worthwhile reads. Some stories, especially in the short short fiction, will succeed despite lack of plot, character, punctuation, what-have-you.

 We may purchase dark fantasy, but try not to publish pure horror. We don't mind feeling the flush of arousal, but will not publish erotica."

"Guns a-blazing might make our day, but we don't suspect most military SF will win us over. Humor? We take it, it often works especially for short short fiction, but do keep in mind that one alien's funny bone is located near another species' sac of indifference. We're likely not your best market for longer funny tales."

I've never sent a story to *Daily Science Fiction*. (Yet)

Submit here:
https://dailysciencefiction.com/submit/story/guidelines

54

ARSENIKA

peculative Poetry & Flash Fiction

Editor: S.Qiouyi Lu
    Pay: $60 fiction $30 poetry
    Word range: up to 1,000
    Simultaneous submissions? Yes
    Reprints? No
    Ezine - Based out of US (Los Angeles)

Arsenika was created in December 2016 and is a journal of speculative poetry and flash fiction.

The editor and creator of this project, S. Qiouyi Lu is a speculative fiction writer and has been featured in many of the markets listed in this guide, such as *Clarkesworld, Cast of Wonders, Uncanny,* and *The Magazine of Fantasy & Science Fiction.*

From the website:

"Arsenika looks for gorgeous, emotional writing: poetry that shimmers with multiple layers of meaning, prose that explores and interrogates.

From hard science fiction to the lightest of magical realism, Arsenika is not bound by genre, though we do prefer the speculative."

I've received my four rejections in less than a month for every story I've submitted. Here is the typical response:

"Thank you for submitting "This Cat Needs a Hat" to Arsenika. Unfortunately, we have decided not to accept this piece for publication. Editor tastes vary widely, and we hope you find a home for this piece soon."

"This Cat Needs a Hat" is still looking for a home. Anyone looking for a misogynist talking feline?

Submit here:
https://arsenika.ink/submissions/

55

THE ARCANIST

cience Fiction, Fantasy & Horror

Editor: Patrick Morris
   Pay: $50
   Word range: 1,000 or less
   Simultaneous submissions? Yes
   Reprints? No
   Ezine and Podcast- Based out of the US

The Arcanist has been going strong for over two years and is an interesting venue for short fiction. They pay well and publish content on a weekly basis (every Friday).
   From the website:

"We strongly believe that fantasy and sci-fi are two of the most important genres in the literary world, helping us escape to distant lands, reflect on our shared humanity, and gaze into the future. We want to provide readers snippets of the genres they love and we want to give writers of these genres a paid place to publish their work. (That's right, we pay you.)"

The editors define a good story on Littsburgh.com:

> The very best SFF stories combine imaginative world-building elements with hardened, time-honored storytelling techniques, which is obviously a lot easier said than done

(especially in under 1K words!).
We get a lot of stories that have a great premise or an imaginative world where we find ourselves in awe that someone actually thought them up. Then you get through the piece and there's no character growth, no choices being made, no movement, and those are vital for a story of any genre to succeed. A good story will have active characters, a fully constructed plot, etc.

> A good SFF story will have all of the elements that make a lit fiction story tick plus fantastic elements that dazzle us. It's a delicate balance!"

I've submitted five stories here and received my rejections in good time (less than a month). Here is the typical letter I've received:

"Thanks for giving us the chance to read The Foreign Student. After careful consideration, we are unfortunately going to pass at this time. If you have other works that you think might be a good fit for The Arcanist, we encourage you to submit them through our Google form. We look forward to reading more of your work in the future and hope that this piece finds a home as well."

I self-published "The Foreign Student" as "The Lore of Lust" after failing to find it a home.

∽

Submit here:
https://thearcanist.io/tag/submission-guidelines/

56

DREAM OF SHADOWS

antasy & Horror

Editor: Filipe Lichtenheld
 Pay: 20 Euros
 Word range: max 1,500
 Simultaneous submissions? Yes
 Reprints? No
 Ezine and Print- Based out of UK

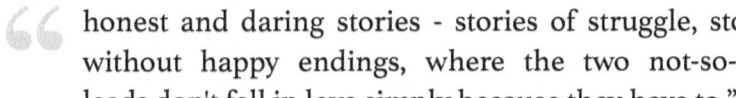

Dream of Shadows comes from the city of Jack the Ripper (London, England) and wants to offer readers:

> " honest and daring stories - stories of struggle, stories without happy endings, where the two not-so-sexy leads don't fall in love simply because they have to."

One short story is featured on the website every month. The website says:

"We're not too fond of science-fiction. While we will sometimes consider stories of something coming down to Earth from another planet if the focus is horror or fantasy, we're not really looking for space adventures.

> We particularly like honest and daring stories with strong characters pursuing goals, although we recognize that if a story is good, it's good.

We're realists, so we don't need a happy ending. Send us those stories that other publishers rejected because they were too dark.
Having said that, we don't want stories with gratuitous and/or over-the-top sex, violence or swearing. And it should go without saying, but we won't allow discrimination either.
On a similar note, we're also not very fond of preachy stories, where one character explains to another how terrible humans are. We get it, people suck."

The editor provides extra tips of what he is looking for:
Stuff we like :

- a good old tale of a character who wants something and tries to get it, meeting obstacles along the way
- prose that grabs us and moves us and makes us feel for and with the character
- supernatural elements. While we personally like a good serial killer or coming-of-age story, Dream of Shadows is all about that supernatural stuff
- Stuff we're not too fond of
- stories where the character doesn't want anything or woe-

The Guide of All Guides

is-me stories where the character spends most of the time complaining, without doing anything to change it
- second-person narration. It just sounds too much like meditation tapes or choose-your-own-adventure games to us. Sorry
- pieces that are too experimental, like stream-of-consciousness stories or stories told from really odd points of view (like a flower or a walking stick) or stories that are basically just descriptions
- romance. We don't mind if love or a relationship is used to drive inner conflict, as long as it's not the focus of the story."

I've submitted five stories to this market and have received standard rejection letters either on the same day, or at most, in a day or two.

"Thank you for submitting your story, THIS CAT NEEDS A HAT, to Dream of Shadows. Unfortunately, we have decided not to publish it. But we wish you best success selling this story in the future."

"This Cat Needs a Hat" and my anti-hero who offends a witch and is transformed into a house cat is still looking for a venue.

Submit here:
https://www.dreamofshadows.co.uk/submission-guidelines

57

SCIPHI JOURNAL

*I*dea-Driven Science Fiction

Editor: Adam Gerencser & M. M. Rodriguez
    Pay: 3 Euros per word
    Word range: under 2,000
    Simultaneous submissions? Yes
    Reprints? No
    Ezine - Australia, now in Europe

The editors of the *SciPhi Journal* describe it as...

> spec fic's smoky village tavern, far from the din of the early 21st century, where professors, nerds and wayfarers rub shoulders and down a few pints on a Friday evening while engaging in flights of fancy, only to sober up again the next morning.

Most publications are asking for "character-driven" fiction, but Sci Phi Journal adamantly does not want that kind of story.

The website explains:

"We are not interested in stories predominantly about the sentiments and subjective experiences of fictional people.

> We want hard SF that zooms out of the personal and lifts off into the structural, the systemic, the epic.

We yearn for carefully crafted philosophical speculation that puzzles over the questions of the future and alternate pasts. And we have a soft spot for stories created as 'artifacts' (fictional, 'in-universe' non-fiction)."

This is what the *SciPhi Journal* is looking for:

- Campbellian hard SF. Reaching back to the roots of classic sci-fi, these rigorous tales take themselves seriously and push the boundaries of our scientific imagination, scaling from the nano to the meta. The cast, if any, is functional and disposable.

> It's the sociological, technological and indeed cosmic developments that sweep the reader up in an expanding sense of wonder.

  - (For a contemporary long-form example that received mainstream attention, see the latter two books of Cixin Liu's Three-Body Problem trilogy.)
  - Fictional non-fiction. The purest, most intimate form of world-building. A transcript of the last UN Security Council meeting before an extinction-level event. The dental bills of a cybernetic vampire. Interviews with eyewitnesses of a battle between Martians and archangels.

(Epistolary fiction falls within this category, though we encourage you to interpret it more broadly, across the full spectrum of artifact fiction.) Think 'World War Z', not 'Walking Dead'."

They are VERY serious about their word counts. I submitted a story that was a few hundred words over, and received this:

"Once upon a time
Your story we hath received,
Excitedly we leapt,
Only to feel slightly peeved.
(For, alas, it would appear,
You had missed our guidelines to read.)
We are but mere mortals
With limited time to spare.
Of works longer than 2000 words
We must sadly beware.
For briefer entreaties
Next time one hopes,
Till then we remain,
Speculatively yours,
the SPJ co-editors.
PS: No offence intended, just an attempt at a wee bit of levity, to share a smile and encourage you to submit again next season - but please do cast a more attentive glance at our submission guidelines."

Submit here:
https://www.sciphijournal.org/index.php/submission-guidelines/

58

FLASH POINT SCIENCE FICTION

cience Fiction & Fantasy

Editor: Thomas J. Griffen
   Pay: $15
   Word range: 100-1,000
   Simultaneous submissions? No
   Reprints? No
   Ezine - Based out of the US

Flash Point Science Fiction is looking for all kinds of fantasy, including grim dark, magical realism, epic, adventure, urban, etc. Plus, they will consider every kind of science fiction like hard, space opera, near future, cyber punk dystopian, and science fantasy. Slipstream and seasonal themes are also welcome. This is a start-up project and it will be interesting to watch the evolution.

From the website:

"Do you love science fiction and fantasy? Us too, but as much as we enjoy the sprawling epics for which our genre is famous (read: infamous), we think there should be more space for the short stuff.

> Stories you can knock out over your morning coffee, or during your lunch break. Stories you don't need a bookmark for."

"So, why Flash Point SF? Because we know there are a lot of wonderful science fiction and fantasy flash stories being written, but the market to publish them is small. That's where we come in. Our goal is to help the market grow and provide SF&F flash authors with a new venue to publish their work."

I have submitted one story to this market, and after reading this note, I am going to completely rewrite this piece.

"Thank you for giving us the opportunity to read "The Morgue Mystery." Unfortunately, it does not meet our needs at this time.

> This story reminded me of the first Men In Black movie

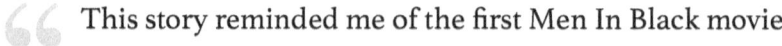

(in a good way), but felt too much like the set up to a longer story. Typically, we prefer stories with a more complete narrative arc, so it's a pass this time, but we wish you luck placing it elsewhere.
We appreciate your interest in Flash Point SF and hope you'll keep us in mind in the future."

"The Morgue Mystery" is still looking for a home and I am actively adding in odd aliens.

∼

Submit here:
https://flashpointsf.com/submissions/

PART III
PODCASTS

59
CAST OF WONDERS

Young Adult Speculative Fiction

Editor: Katherine Inskip
  Pay: 8 cents per word
  Word range: up to 6,000
  Simultaneous submissions? Yes
  Reprints? No
  Podcast - Based out of the US

Cast of Wonders is a fantastic podcast and part of the Escape Artists family. It has been around since 2011, and they pay their writers well while offering the stories for free. This is one of my favorite audio choices while driving in the car.

From the website they are looking for:

"Stories that evoke a sense of wonder, have deep emotional resonance, and have something unreal about them. We aim for a 12-17 age range: that means sophisticated, non-condescending stories with wide appeal, and without gratuitous or explicit sex, violence or pervasive obscene language."

Think Harry Potter or The Hunger Games."

"Stories are presented in audio format, which means our audience rarely skim past boring bits. We're looking for fiction with strong pacing, well-defined characters, engaging dialogue, and clear action. We like a proper narrative structure and a prose style not laden with clichés and over-worn idioms.

We like fiction that makes us think, but the main elements should be thrilling entertainment, adventure and emotional connection. "

"We like all forms of fantasy — high, modern, urban, alternative history, etc. We're less fond of the complex, intricate or cerebral forms of fantasy more common in novel markets; short stories rarely offer enough room to sufficiently develop. We like all forms of science fiction — far-future, near future, space opera, "hard" sci-fi — but it must be accessible to our target audience, meaning a minimum of technical jargon.

Our horror offerings tend to be psychological, comedic, or situational — not visceral."

"We're happy to read comedy, steampunk, age-appropriate paranormal romance, superheroes and many other genres. All that matters is adherence to our core concept and that critical spark of wonder."

The Guide of All Guides

I've found their rejections to be very helpful. Here is one of the two I've received:

"Thank you for sending us "The Versa Vice". We appreciate the chance to read it. Unfortunately, the piece is not for us. Our readers felt the story was missing the developed sense of wonder or fantastic element that we consider the hallmark of Cast of Wonders stories.

> We didn't find the ending as unexpected as we would have liked, and thought some of the character tropes chosen were a little over-used.

If you are still searching for a podcast or magazine to publish this story, you can find a list of recommend venues on our website under Markets. And say hello for us!"

"The Versa Vice" (after being rejected five times by other markets) found a home with Flying Ketchup Press in *Tales from the Dream Zone*. You can read about that tale's journey in *The Story Behind The Stories*.

Submit here:
https://www.castofwonders.org/submissions/

60

PODCASTLE

antasy

Editor: Jen R. Albert & Cherai Clark
  Pay: 8 cents per word
  Word range: up to 6,000
  Simultaneous submissions? Yes
  Reprints? Yes
  Podcast - based out of the US

Podcastle is part of the Escape Artists family and focuses on all subgenres of fantasy. It was launched in April, 2008.
  From the website:

  PodCastle is looking for fantasy stories.

"We're open to all the sub-genres of fantasy, from magical realism to urban fantasy to slipstream to high fantasy, and everything in between.

Fantastical or non-real content should be meaningful to the story. Our word count limit is 6,000. Please note that for original stories, the closer to the limit the story is, the more difficult it is for us to buy it.

 Our "sweet spot" for story length is between 3,000 and 4,500 words."

"We are an audio magazine. Our audience can't skim past the boring parts. Ideally, fiction should have strong pacing, well-defined characters, engaging dialogue, clear action, and still be beautiful. Above all, we're looking for stories that are fun to listen to. Humor is encouraged."

I sent in a story about a pot-smoking, trouble making fairy, and they rejected it with this note:

"Thank you very much for submitting "High Adventure" to us. It's an interesting story (and the Rasta Fairy dialogue was clear), but it didn't quite come together for us and we've decided to pass on it."

"High Adventure" found a home with *Econoclash Magazine* after being passed over by ten previous markets.

Submit here:
https://podcastle.org/guidelines/

61

PSUEDOPOD

Horror

Editor: Shawn Garrett & Alex Hofelich
   Pay: 8 cents per word
   Word range: 1,500 - 6,000
   Simultaneous submissions? Yes
   Reprints: Yes
   Podcast - Based out of US

Psuedopod is looking for quality horror stories and is part of the Escape Artists family. They have been around since 2006 and warn they are for mature audiences only.

From the website:

We're looking for horror: dark, weird fiction. We run the spectrum from grim realism or crime drama, to magic-realism, to blatantly supernatural dark fantasy.

> We publish highly literary stories reminiscent of Poe or Lovecraft as well as vulgar shock-value pulp fiction.

We don't split hairs about genre definitions, and we do not observe any taboos about what kind of content can appear in our stories.

> Originality demands that you're better off avoiding vampires, zombies, and other recognizable horror tropes unless you have put a very unique spin on them."

"What matters most is that the stories are dark and compelling. Since we're an audio magazine, our audience can't skim past the boring parts, so stories with beautiful language at the expense of plot don't translate well."

> We're looking for fiction with strong pacing, well-defined characters, engaging dialogue, and clear action."

It can be beautiful too, if you've got all those other bases covered. Dark humor is just fine, and we run it on occasion; but we are more interested in tragedy than comedy, and comedy is better received the more sick and morbid it is. Above all, we want stories that make us think, that stick with us, that make us catch ourselves checking the locks a second time before bed."

I've sent them five stories, and they sometimes send back very helpful notes.

Here is one:

"Thank you for submitting "The Writing Retreat" to us. It's an interesting story, but it didn't quite come together for us and we've decided to pass on it. The piece contained a nice amount of humor, and the writing is clear and easy to visualize. However, the zombie story is a familiar one.

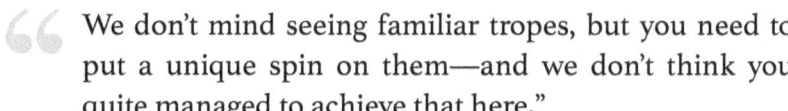

We don't mind seeing familiar tropes, but you need to put a unique spin on them—and we don't think you quite managed to achieve that here."

"The Writing Retreat" was published in *Strangely Funny VII* (after being rejected approximately 10 times by other markets). You can read about the shuffle step of these zombies to print in *The Publishers Behind the Pages*.

And this one was entertaining and gave me hope:

"Thank you very much for submitting "The Last Ride" to us. It's an interesting story, but it didn't quite come together for us and we've decided to pass on it.

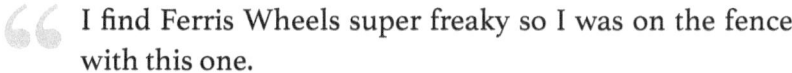

I find Ferris Wheels super freaky so I was on the fence with this one.

But in the end the buildup was too slow for a story so short, so I had to pass. I love your writing style, however. Please consider us again in the future."

"The Last Ride" was picked up by *The Corona Book of Short Stories* (after being rejected five times.) More details on that how that happened in *The Story Behind The Stories*.

∽

Submit here:
https://pseudopod.org/submissions/

62

ESCAPE POD

cience Fiction

Editor: S.B. Divya & Mur Lafferty
  Pay: 8 cents per word
  Word range: 600-6,000
  Simultaneous submissions? Yes
  Reprints? Yes
  Podcast - based out of the US

Escape Pod has been around since 2005 and is part of the Escape Artists Family. They gear their content towards adult listeners.
  From the website:

> "Escape Pod is a science fiction market. We are fairly flexible on what counts as science (we'll delve into superheroes or

steampunk on occasion) and are interested in exploring the range of the genre".

> We want stories that center on science, technology, future projections, and/or alternate history, and how any or all of these things intersect with people.

"We publish our stories in text and audio, but audio is our primary format. Because our audience cannot easily reread or skim, we prefer stories of high clarity and tight pacing. Typographic novelties (e.g., footnotes) are difficult for us to publish."

I sent them a story about a leech man who falls in love with a cop while they try and solve a series of vampire-like murders. Here is my rejection:

"Thank you for sending "Shafted" to Escape Pod. Unfortunately, this story wasn't a good fit for us. Choosing stories is a subjective process, and we have to reject many well-written stories. We wish you the best in finding this a good home and look forward to your next submission.

> This story had a fun premise, but we had trouble believing the backstory, and the dialogue didn't always ring true to us."

"Shafted" is in the process of being turned into a paranormal romance novel.

∼

Submit here:
https://escapepod.org/guidelines/short-fiction/

63
THE OTHER STORIES

*H*orror, Sci-Fi & Thriller

Editor: Kez the Editor
   Pay: $10
   Word range: must be 2,000
   Simultaneous submissions? Yes
   Reprints? Yes
   Podcast - Based out of the UK

This is one of my favorite markets and communities. *The Other Stories* podcast is a project by Hawk & Cleaver and they are fun and responsive. I often listen to their creepy short stories when I am in the car.

> *These aren't the stories your mother used to tell you ... no, these are The Other Stories.*

ANGELIQUE FAWNS

The Other Stories is a weekly short story podcast. A modern take on The Twilight Zone, Tales From The Crypt, or The Outer Limits. Sci-Fi, Horror, Thriller, WTF stories delivered right to your podcast feed every Monday morning.

The submissions page says:

> If you think you've got what it takes to terrify, scar and haunt our audience of 10,000 daily listeners, then we want your stories!
>
> If accepted, we'll get our fantastic narration team to lend their voices, our editor will sprinkle some magic pixie dust on the track, and you could have your story heard by thousands of listeners each week."

They've even purchased one of my pieces. To submit to *The Other Stories*, your piece must fit one of their upcoming themes. I wrote a piece about a woman stuck in an immersion chamber in response to a call for stories about "Silence".

Listen to MGS04 here

From there I discovered their other podcasts: *Horror Hangout; Great Writers Share; The Story Studio;* and *Miscreation*. They are all entertaining. I also love their Facebook page.

Even though they have sent me five rejections, the tone of them is always encouraging. Here is one for "The Black Hole of Enlightenment" (still not picked up):

> "Thanks for this. Although we did enjoy it, the ending didn't quite come together as strongly as we would've liked. We won't be running this one but would love to see more of your work."

And another for "The New Mutants" (bought by Third Flatiron Publishing):

"Thanks for sending this story in! We always enjoy reading one of your stories when they come in. We think you've got a terrific voice! Unfortunately, this story didn't quite land as strongly with some of our readers as the others so we're going to pass on this one. I'd love to see more of your stuff, though, so please keep writing!!!"

Submit here:
https://theotherstories.net/submissions

64

THE OVERCAST

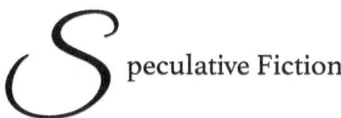peculative Fiction

Editor: J.S. Arquin
  Pay: $20
  Word range: 1,000 - 5,000
  Simultaneous submissions? Yes
  Reprints? Yes
  Podcast - Based out of the US

The Overcast is a speculative fiction podcast and likes to features writers from the Pacific Northwest. J.S. Arquin is from Portland, Oregon.

The Overcast is run by one man and he explains:

"Every other week we produce short stories in an easy to digest audio format, perfect for listening to while driving, biking, jogging, riding a unicycle, or striding across the land perched atop your giant killer robot. Listening while swimming is not advised."

Here is some information from the website:

"We are interested in speculative fiction, whatever that means to you, be it Science Fiction, Fantasy, Steampunk, Magical Realism, Slipstream, or an as-yet-unnamed genre. Anything that looks at the world and life from an unexpected angle. We want the original vision of William Gibson. The magic and beauty of Erin Morgenstern. The uncompromising voice of Margaret Atwood. The technical brilliance of Ted Chiang."

 We want to read stories that transport us to places that we've never imagined."

"We want to still be thinking about a story days after reading it. Be original. Be amazing."

I've submitted one story to them:

"Thank you for the opportunity to read "Planet Nine". Unfortunately, the story didn't fit our current needs. Best of luck placing it elsewhere. Thank you for taking the time to submit to The Overcast."

"Planet Nine" was rejected 10x and became one of my first published stories when it was picked up by *The Gateway Review: A Journal of Magical Realism*. You can learn more about it in *The Story Behind The Stories*.

Submit here:
https://theovercast.libsyn.com/submissions-guidelines

65

NOSLEEP

Horror

Editor: David Cummings
  Pay: $100 - $125 US
  Word range: 1,200 - no max
  Simultaneous submissions? Yes
  Reprints? Yes
  Podcast - Based out of US

NoSleep is an esteemed market for horror writers, and has an avid following for the podcast and on reddit. Here is a bit about the history from their website:

"In the spring of 2010, a new forum appeared on Reddit.com. It was called "Nosleep" and the concept of this forum (or "subreddit") was to be a place for people to post original scary stories about frightening experiences."

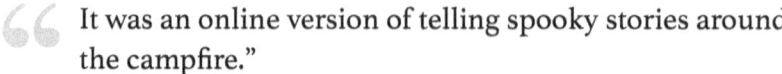 It was an online version of telling spooky stories around the campfire."

"A year later, as Nosleep was growing at a rapid pace, one member named Matt Hansen proposed the idea of doing a podcast where some of the top stories from Nosleep would be narrated in audiobook style. The response was quite positive and over the next few months a small group of members endeavored to put together what would come to be known as The Nosleep Podcast. On June 13th, 2011 Episode #1 was released.
David Cummings assumed the role of host and producer and it was decided to release a new episode every two weeks. Producing the podcast has been a learning experience from the start with many Redditors volunteering to narrate and help produce the shows."

I've sent them two stories "The Rougarou" and "The Black Hole of Enlightenment" and waited five months to over a year for my responses. Here is the form rejection I received:

"Thank you for your submission. Unfortunately, it's not quite right for the podcast so we'll be passing on using it, but please don't hesitate to send us more in future!"

"The Rougarou" was published by Soteira Press in *The Monsters We Forgot Vol. 3*, and The Black Hole of Enlightenment is homeless.

Submit here:
https://www.thenosleeppodcast.com/submissions

66
GALLERY OF CURIOSITIES

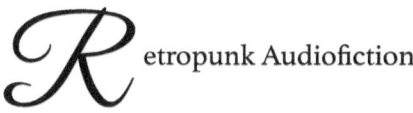etropunk Audiofiction

Editor: Kevin Frost
    Pay: 4 cents per word
    Word range: up to 7500
    Simultaneous submissions? No
    Reprints? Yes, 1 cent per word
    eBook, Print & Podcast - Based out of the US

This venue publishes a short story collection *Curiosities* two to three times a year, in both digital and print, and runs a podcast called *Gallery of Curiosities* which features stories from the publication. They call themselves:

> *A comfortable two-headed beast at play in the curious and often dark corners of retropunk fiction. That means*

steampunk, dieselpunk, dreadpunk, bronzepunk, others that haven't even been invented yet punk ... but not atompunk. Sorry, space fans, we draw our line at Sputnik.

Keeping in mind that audio is their focus they ask for:

"Stories that entertain.

We want to be taken on an adventure in a time that never was,

be it steampunk, gaslamp, weird tales, dreadpunk, vintage horror, new weird, mad science, fantastic cities (please!), monsters, impossible machines, clockworks, alt-history adventures, surprises, weird westerns, and things that shouldn't work."

I've sent them two stories and received rejections in a couple of days.

"Thanks again for your time and story. This one isn't feeling like a good match for us."

"The Museum of the Lost People" is still lost.
"A Tasty Festival" is about a Ferris Wheel that eats children and it lives in the anthology *Demonic Carnival*. You can read more about its journey in *The Story Behind The Stories*.

Submit here:
https://gallerycurious.com/fiction/

ACKNOWLEDGMENTS

So many friends and family helped me bring this project to completion. My husband Luke Fawns and daughter Faith basically gave me up for several months while I spent every spare moment creating this guide. My mother edited each version with pointed precision and no-nonsense advice. Sway Benoit, my lovely sister-in-law (and fellow speculative fiction writer) also donated many hours of her time helping me with consistency, formatting and content. Kim Fehr is an exceptional editor and fellow writer. I'd like to give special thanks to all the editors and publishers in this guide who gave me permission to use their rejection letters. Without angels like them, donating hours upon hours of their time, new writers would have no place to learn and get published. Happy writing everyone!

ABOUT THE AUTHOR

Angelique Fawns is a journalist and speculative fiction writer. She began her career writing articles about naked cave dwellers in Tenerife, Canary Islands, and hosting a radio show in Mooloolaba, Australia. Now she works full-time making television commercials for Global TV in Toronto. She writes fiction for fun and uses her journalism skills to promote editors, publishers and authors. She lives on a farm north of the city with her husband, daughter, horses, goats, chickens, and a Potcake rescue dog.

Find out more at www.fawns.ca

ALSO BY ANGELIQUE FAWNS

The Story Behind The Stories

The Publishers Behind The Pages

If you enjoyed this guide and would like to dive deeper into selling your stories, check out the next two volumes in this series.

Read the actual stories and find out why publishers bought them.

Hear from from the editors themselves and get the inside scoop on why they do what they do.

Learn how many rejections it took before each story sold.

Best yet, read the actual rejection letters!

Learn how they went from some of the sharp statements below to a successful sale...

"The piece made no sense"

"How does the 'magic' work, and why isn't there a major investigation going on in a town where 50 some kids have gone missing?"

"Let's skip for a moment in the lack of plausibility... By the time the story seems to be going somewhere, the story ends."

www.ingramcontent.com/pod-product-compliance
Lightning Source LLC
Chambersburg PA
CBHW030904080526
44589CB00010B/145